D0465202

October BM

The Aesthetic Thought of the French Enlightenment

The Aesthetic Thought of the French Enlightenment

Francis X. J. Coleman

University of Pittsburgh Press

Library of Congress Catalog Card Number 76-136570
ISBN 0–8229–3221–0
Copyright © 1971, University of Pittsburgh Press
Henry M. Snyder & Co., Inc., London
Manufactured in the United States of America

FOR KINGSLEY BLAKE PRICE

Nous n'acquérons guère de connaissances
nouvelles que pour nous désabuser de
quelque illusion agréable.

d'Alembert

Contents

Preface

IT IS always wise to describe as soon as possible what sort of book one is proposing to the reader. Although one risks turning away a great many readers at the door, at least those who enter do so without false expectations.

I have not undertaken to write a history of aesthetic thought during the French Enlightenment; books and monographs already exist on that subject in several languages. However, my own study could not be altogether nonhistorical because, among other things, I have tried to give the contours and changes of French aesthetic thought during the eighteenth century. And so the reader will find references to dates and sometimes to social or political events.

Secondly, I have not undertaken to write an intellectual history, or a history of ideas, of French aesthetics. Again, this sort of thing has been done by many other writers and done well. *Entre le classicisme et le romantisme* by Wladyslaw Folkierski naturally comes to mind. Like all good intellectual histories, it crosses national boundaries and traces the influence of French, English, German, and Italian aestheticians upon one another. However, my own study is not altogether bereft of what I might call historicism. From time to time I have traced the ways in which a certain writer influenced another in regard to a certain doctrine, but I have always done so as an aside.

And to keep the asides from getting out of hand, I have arbitrarily confined myself to the French.

Thirdly, I have not tried to make a synthesis, which is one of the most voguish words in the academic world, of French thought on aesthetics during the eighteenth century; this would not only have been pointless but also impossible. I suppose that those who seek a synthesis or a homogeneous spirit of an age will always find it, but then, of course, one can establish any thesis by picking and choosing among the data. Because generalities about French thought on the fine arts during the Enlightenment tend to be hollow and unhelpful, I have tried to avoid them. However, in dealing with certain topics, I could not always avoid forcing a certain contrast or similarity, for I have tried to make as clear and comprehensible as possible the thought of almost thirty aestheticians of the French Enlightenment.

Fourth and lastly, I have not attempted to write a history of the art of the eighteenth century. Not only would that require a dozen volumes, but they would have to be written by a team of specialists in music, literature, painting, and architecture. However, just as there is no such thing as philosophy *tout court*—though, of course, there have been many attempts at purely speculative philosophy—but only philosophy *of* (for example, the philosophy of science, or of history, or of moral behavior) so, too, it would be idle to attempt a study of the French aestheticians of the Enlightenment without a fair acquaintance with the fine arts of the eighteenth century. And so the reader will find several references to particular works of art in the study that is to follow, sometimes to illustrate aesthetic theories of that period, sometimes to provide a background or décor for certain eighteenth-century attitudes.

After so many warnings about what the reader is not to expect, I should like to make it clear, in general outline, what he is to expect. There exist a fairly large number of writings on the fine arts that have never, to the best of my knowledge, been subjected to a critical or philosophical analysis. Unlike the writings of Descartes, Malebranche, and Pascal, whose ideas have been deftly analyzed by generations of persons interested in philosophy, the writings of Batteux, Crousaz, André, Dubos, and many others have often been acknowledged in histories of criticism and the fine arts but have never been closely scrutinized. They have been like undistinguished guests invited to a distinguished ball—people might have noticed their presence, but no one thought it worth the trouble to get to know them. I have tried to make clear what their theories about the fine arts were and, more importantly, to show their philosophical motivations. It is, of course, true that one can explain why a man wrote what he did from a number of different points of view; one might attempt a psychological analysis of certain philosophical writings or perhaps a purely economic explanation. These various points of view doubtless have their place. But in this study I have attempted to confine myself to a philosophical analysis of eighteenth-century French aesthetics, that is, to show the assumptions that various thinkers made either tacitly or overtly, to reveal what must have been the model or metaphor upon which they were relying if certain of their ideas are to be taken seriously, and to explain why certain of their ideas lead nowhere or perhaps to something of considerable interest. In short, I have attempted not only to explain but to interpret and to evaluate.

Along with the unknown writers of the French Enlightenment, I have also devoted considerable attention to the aesthetic theories of Diderot. Here I can hardly pique myself on cultivating virgin soil. No other aesthetician of the Enlightenment has received so much attention, yet I hope that my interpretations of his theories are both new and helpful. Above all, I have tried to show how his thought contrasts with and explains certain of the ideas of the lesser-known French aestheticians.

Anyone acquainted with eighteenth-century French literature might wonder at the outset how so many writers on the fine arts could be compressed and subjected to analysis in such a short volume as this. Surely there were as many writers on the fine arts as there were on ethics during the period. It took L. G. Crocker two robust volumes, *An Age of Crisis* and *Nature and Culture*,[1] to present a thorough account of the ethical thought of the Enlightenment. I should like to answer this objection before beginning the study, and to do so I shall draw a distinction between aesthetic theories and critical theories. As I have already implied, my chief interest in this study lies in aesthetic theories.

There are many precedents for distinguishing aesthetic from critical theories. Saintsbury, for example, in the introduction to his *History of Criticism and Literary Taste*,[2] states that he will avoid philosophical or aesthetic treatises and confine himself to criticism. He does not, however, make clear in what the distinction consists. And one must admit that though one can almost always *feel* the difference between the two, it is not so simple to *explain* it. Even so, the chief differences seem to be the following:

1. Critical theories tend to be revelations of one's own sensibility and of one's personal commitments. Consequently, a critical theory is persuasive in tone and sometimes almost an apologia. The critic has certain strong feelings about what art "really" is or ought to be, and he does his best, with all the blandishments of style, wit, and sometimes even with threats, to persuade other persons to adopt his point of view. Aesthetic theories, however, attempt to analyze impartially and impersonally the central ideas that one encounters in the fine arts, such as "artistic value," "standards of taste," "beauty," and "work of art." It goes without saying that the aesthetician would be greatly pleased if other persons would agree with his analyses and explications, but when one "agrees" with a critical theory, it would be more precise to say that one has allied oneself to it, committed oneself to it, or perhaps been wooed by it. But when one agrees with an aesthetic theory, it is rather that

one believes it to be true, or that one finds it to be an accurate explication of the matter in hand. I do not mean to imply that one never encounters a sort of mixed discourse—half criticism and half aesthetics—for sometimes in giving a critical account of a certain work of art, or of a kind of art, the critic is insensibly led to certain philosophical or aesthetic arguments to support or clarify his critical attitude. Even so, with a bit of semantic surgery one can distinguish the two varieties of discourse.

2. Critical theories have sometimes a didactic end, sometimes a practical end: didactic in that the critic wants the public to see art or nature in a new way; practical in that he wants artists to fashion a new kind of art. Rousseau, for example, tried to teach his contemporaries to appreciate the wildness, disorder, and sublimity of nature. For better or worse, he succeeded to a large degree. The exquisite balance of the classical garden gradually gave way to the shaggy confusion of the garden *à l'anglaise*. Other critics of the period tried to persuade artists to *de-Romanize* their works, to look to the schools of the north, and to develop a style peculiarly French. Aesthetic theories, however, have neither a practical nor a didactic end; they seek only to illuminate.

3. Critical theories, so to speak, ride the waves. They have their periods of ascent, their moments in the sun when both the artists and the public are greatly taken with them, and then the vogue passes. One thinks of the rise, crest, and descent of the return to the antique during the last third of the eighteenth century and the beginning of the nineteenth. Aesthetic theories, however, influence neither artists nor the public; they might fall into desuetude, or they might propagate themselves in the minds of other philosophers. Aesthetic theories hold their own in proportion to the evidence advanced for them or, to speak more precisely, in proportion to what one believes to be adequate reason for espousing them.

After this brief digression, it may be more understandable

how I have dealt with so many writers on the fine arts in so little space. In France, at least, before 1700 there were abundant critical and artistic theories—treatises on architecture, on music, on painting, dozens of *ars poeticas*, apologies for the theatre—but there were no aesthetic theories. I hasten to make one exception—Descartes. There are a few passages in his writings which are clearly in the domain of aesthetics. But though a number of treatises have been written on Descartes's aesthetics, I am afraid that they are more the product of ingenious interpretation and critical exuberance than of theories actually held by Descartes. But be that as it may, it was not until the end of the reign of Louis XIV that philosophical aesthetics began to appear in France. Although the treatises were often a medley of psychology, crude physics, and medicine, there does appear a new strain—an analytic and philosophical reflection upon the fine arts. Certain writers were no longer content with dithyrambic accounts of personal likes and dislikes, interlaced with quotations from the Greek and Latin poets.

It is on the basis of the distinction that I have drawn between critical and aesthetic theories that I have been able to overlook and ignore a number of writers on the fine arts during the French Enlightenment. Moreover, the same distinction has enabled me to skirt a great many of the writings of such persons as Diderot, Voltaire, Fénelon, and Marmontel. Although I am convinced that the distinction I have drawn between critical and aesthetic theories is far from being verbal or academic, I must leave the reader to decide that issue for himself.

The same distinction has also allowed me to avoid a number of entanglements such as the Quarrel Between the Ancients and Moderns. It might have been the Quarrel that helped bring about philosophical reflection upon the fine arts; it might also have been that the Quarrel was a natural result of Cartesianism; and it might have been that in some sense the Moderns won the Quarrel because of their reliance upon the Cartesian notion of progress. In any event, it is a quarrel that I am very happy to have the philosophical right to ignore, for there is surely no more boring or puerile episode in the history of French literature.

It might not be amiss to say a few words about the form of the writings of the eighteenth-century aestheticians. With the notable exceptions of Crousaz, Batteux, and Condillac, French aestheticians of the period were not systematic thinkers. The very elegant writer Trublet in his *Essais sur divers sujets de littérature*[3] contrasts the manner of writing by unrelated thoughts or *aperçus* with that of building systems:

> There are happy moments in life that never return.
> During a heated conversation, the ideas of other persons
> sometimes bring to birth ideas or thoughts that one
> would search for in vain in one's study, and when
> one's mind is at rest. . . . What is it in a work that
> gives pleasure to a man of intelligence? It is what
> illuminates him, makes him think . . . but often in
> heavy volumes [Trublet has in mind methodical and
> systematic works] he finds only a few ideas of this sort.[4]

Trublet hastens to add that perhaps those who write without having a system are lazy or lack logical rigor or application, but he rightly points out that such writers are not therefore lacking in fecundity, invention, and perception. He continues:

> Transitions are the most common source of stylistic
> languor; one would greatly abridge many systematic
> works, without losing anything essential to the subject,
> if one cut out everything that the author set down
> simply to join together his ideas and to give a certain
> form to his work.[5]

As one reads many of the French aestheticians of the period one might be tempted to dismiss them with a nod or a smile. One might assume that since their language is antiquated their ideas must be so as well, or that since the civilization that produced them was overcome by the Revolution their doctrines must no longer be relevant, or that since none of these writers were professional philosophers their works must be elementary and confused. However, just as the fine arts in France during the first two-thirds of the eighteenth century tend to suggest rather than to assert, to move by nuance rather than by bold steps, so, too, many of the French aestheticians of the period hint, give gentle indications, sometimes admit their confusions, but never attempt to erect great systems in the manner of Christian Wolff or A. G. Baumgarten, who were their German contemporaries. Even Batteux and Crousaz, who attempt something approaching synthetic thought on aesthetics, never pursue the subject with that obstinate and pugnacious rigor of such writers as Baumgarten. One is tempted to say that the French writers of the period were too sensitive to the complexities of the fine arts and of the aesthetic life of man to attempt great systems. Nor shall we find the French aestheticians of the period descending into the depths of splendid obscurity which we so often encounter among their German contemporaries.

So much for the form of the writings with which this study deals. I shall now add a word or two about their tone and savor. Just as the fine arts of the *Grand Siècle* had been regal, impersonal, ceremonial, and static, so, too, a great many literary productions of the period were arch and declamatory. The new art of the eighteenth century—painting, literature, furniture, music—was mobile, dynamic, and intimate. From the *Régence* until around 1760, when another tendency to return to the antique occured, artists sought fantasy, intimacy, and humanity in their works. One finds the same tendency among the aestheticians of the period; their writings lose the tone of oratory to find the grace and intimacy of the salon. They wrote, and were satisfied to write, for a small number of persons. Trublet, illustrating a sentiment that Horace had expressed, "Neque te ut miretur turba, labores; contentus paucis lectoribus,"[6] says: "One has to write for everyone if one wants to please everyone; but to arrive at that end one must write less perfectly than if one wrote only for persons of considerable understanding."[7]

I have said that the fine arts of the first two-thirds of the eighteenth century tend to be dynamic, imbued with a sort of exquisite tension; one might also say that they tend to be dualistic. That is to say, in many novels of the period one finds reason opposed to sentiment as in *Les Egarements du coeur et de l'esprit* of Crébillon Fils, or social conventions opposed to personal desires as in *La Vie de Marianne* of Marivaux, or the demands of art opposed to the demands of morality as in the Marquis de Sade. The same dualistic tensions could be traced throughout much of the painting, music, and even furniture of the period. It is not too surprising to find, then, that most of the aestheticians are dualists of one sort or another and that their writings reflect these various tensions. For this reason I have divided my study into four main sections, each of which reflects a major tension in the aesthetic thought of the period: I. Reason and Sentiment, II. Rules and Spontaneity, III. Imitation and Creation, and IV. Art, Language, and Morality. Although these antitheses were seldom explicitly stated by the writers whom we shall be studying, they were, nonetheless, implicit in their thought. These antitheses were, so to speak, the perturbations of sunlight that caused so many minute changes and disturbances in the climate of thought.

And now a final word about undertaking such a study as this. Although the English and German aestheticians of the eighteenth century are well known and have been examined with philosophical care, the French have been neglected. One might justify this study on the grounds of philosophical curiosity; one might simply say that there is a lacuna in the literature. But one might like to add that the age which produced these writers was the apogee of French civilization. During the period from the *Régence* to the Revolution in 1789 the refinements of civilization and the sweetness of life reached their peak not only in France, but in Western civilization. In any event, there are persons who strongly believe this. And so it should not be altogether idle to look carefully into the writings of the aesthetic spokesmen of the age.

Acknowledgments

WITHOUT the kind help of the personnel of the Bibliothèque Nationale of Paris and a grant from the National Endowment for the Humanities, I could never have written this study. I am indebted also to certain philosophers, professors of the fine arts, and artists, both in France and in the United States, who read various parts of the manuscript, but since I should not like any of my errors or indiscretions to be imputed to them, I shall leave them nameless. I must also thank Miss Alice Gay for her indefatigable patience in preparing the manuscript. But chiefly I must thank the philosophy department of the University of Pittsburgh, and Professor Kurt Baier, for making my year's leave of absence possible.

The Aesthetic Thought of the French Enlightenment

I Reason and Sentiment

THROUGHOUT the long history of philosophy there has appeared from time to time a certain dilemma which is both attractive and fatal. One encounters the dilemma in Plato's epistemology, in St. Augustine's philosophy of religion, in Hegel's metaphysics, in Kant's ethics, and in the aesthetics of the French Enlightenment. In general terms the dilemma consists in postulating the existence of two radically different entities which must cooperate with each other or be in touch with each other, so that a certain event can be satisfactorily explained. But if the two entities are essentially different, it follows that there could not be a third entity, partaking of the attributes of the two contraries, which serves as a link or intermediary. Philosophical tenacity must always pay dearly. If one wants to hold that there exist two essentially different sorts of things, and if one also wants to explain a certain mundane event, one will be forced to juggle, camouflage, or invent a contradictory *tertium quid* or to reinterpret the mundane event that one wanted to explain in the first place. In sum, one will have a rash of philosophical difficulties.

To illustrate this sort of dilemma, I should like to turn to Kant's ethics. The mundane fact that Kant wanted to explain was this: it is true that under certain conditions human beings act freely, that is, of their own free will or without being constrained. That this was true appeared incontestable to Kant, and it has appeared so to the bulk of mankind. Though some philosophers have maintained that human freedom is illusory, I shall ignore them, because I want only to illustrate the kind of dilemma that we shall shortly encounter among the French aestheticians.

In addition, Kant also implies that there exist two radically different kinds of entities or, more precisely, two different aspects of any given entity: the noumenon, of which one cannot speak and which by theory can never be the object of scientific investigation, and the phenomenon, which is the outward appearance of the noumenon and the object of empirical investigation. I shall not enter into the intricacies of Kant's explanation of human freedom; however, roughly put, he wants to hold that a certain man, for example Jones, is really a noumenal object, and as such he apprehends the ethical law and acts freely. As a phenomenal object Jones can be studied by the physiologist or psychologist, and all of his behavior is causally determined. Even Jones's thoughts are phenomenal; that is to say, his stream of consciousness is determined by the laws of the association of ideas.

Given these three assumptions: (1) certain persons sometimes act freely, (2) for every object there is a noumenal aspect, and (3) Jones as a phenomenal object is entirely determined, it is obvious that Kant will have insurmountable difficulties. For if one asserts that Jones is really a noumenal object, then Jones could act only freely, and consequently, by the theory, Jones could not do otherwise than obey the moral law. But if it is logically impossible for someone to err morally, it follows that he could not be correctly described as a moral agent. As St. Thomas had mentioned centuries before, it is inappropriate to speak of God as a moral agent because, given His perfect goodness, He cannot act otherwise. On the other hand, if one asserts that Jones is a phenomenal object, then Jones acts neither freely nor unfreely. Given Kant's theory of the phenomenal, one might say that Jones falls into disrepair, like a clock, or breaks a habit, like an ill-trained Viennese dancing horse. In any event, Jones would not be held morally responsible. Therefore one might be tempted to say that there exists a *tertium quid*, a third Jones, partaking of the properties of both the phenomenal and the noumenal, but then one would contradict oneself. Or one might try to maintain that the noumenal Jones gets in touch with the phenomenal Jones, but, given the theory, this would be equally impossible.

I have, perhaps, developed this example at tedious length. A more familiar illustration of the dilemma might be drawn from Christian theology, in which, at least according to St. Augustine and St. Thomas, there exists an eternal and omnipotent God, and a temporal and finite being called man. According to the scheme, the event to be explained is man's apprehension of certain propositions that he could not discover by his own forces, that is, the various articles of the Nicene Creed. Consequently, a third entity had to be invented, partaking both of God's properties and of man's. But since, I trust, that the kind of dilemma which has so frequently occurred in philosophy is now sufficiently clear, I shall not bother to develop this second example but instead turn immediately to the ways in which the dilemma caused so much discomfort and confusion among the French aestheticians of the eighteenth century.

Just as it is difficult for many philosophers of our own day to think about certain philosophical problems without seriously weighing and considering the works of Wittgenstein; so, too, in the first third of the eighteenth century in France, many writers naturally turned to the works of Descartes, sometimes only to sound the note of orthodoxy, sometimes to register complete agreement, but more often to note nuances of change and development. It might be well, consequently, to notice how Descartes, in the *Traité des passions*,[1] in part prepared the way for the dilemma of reason and sentiment that so greatly preoccupied French aestheticians of the period. I should like to

5

mention how the same dilemma and its ancillary crudities plague many philosophers of our own period who have written on ethics and aesthetics, such as Charles Stevenson, but that would be a long and, perhaps, intolerable digression. Reflecting upon the relation of the fine arts and natural beauty to reason and sentiment, Descartes had written:

> We commonly call "good" or "bad" that which our inner sense judges to be helpful or hurtful to our nature, but we call something "beautiful" or "ugly" which is represented by our exterior senses, chiefly that of sight, which is considered the highest. And so it results that there are two species of love, to wit, that which we have for good things, and that which we have for beautiful things; we might call the latter "agreeable" so as not to confound it with the former or with the objects of desire. But what is quite remarkable in this regard is that the feelings of agreeableness and of horror are generally more violent than the other sorts of love and hatred, because that which comes to the soul by means of the exterior senses touches it more strongly than that which is represented to it by the reason, and, in any case, the former have generally less truth; and so it is the case that, of all the feelings, those of the beautiful and the ugly deceive the most and are those against which one must be the most on guard.[2]

That our ideas of the beautiful and the ugly are confused and unreliable, that they are irremediably inferior to our ideas of metaphysics, mathematics, and even ethics, and that they depend solely upon the agreeableness of certain impressions given to the sensitive soul by the senses of sight and hearing— these sparse dicta constituted aesthetic orthodoxy in France at the turn of the seventeenth century. As we shall see, J. P. Crousaz, who was a professor of philosophy and mathematics at the Academy of Lausanne, was to modify and develop these dicta greatly in his *Traité du beau*, which appeared in 1715. This is the first work on philosophical aesthetics, as I defined that term in the Preface, to appear both in France and in the Occident since the late Hellenistic and early Christian eras. Of course one can extrapolate certain aesthetic theories from the works of various medieval philosophers, but there are only a few sentences in the entire corpus of medieval philosophy which are overtly concerned with aesthetics. But since questions of priority or singularity are always a little tedious, I shall confine myself to what is important in the *Traité du beau* of Crousaz.

Though he will greatly modify what might be called Cartesian aesthetics, Crousaz's method is clearly that of Descartes. In the epistolary dedication to the Count du Luc, Crousaz writes:

> I confine myself to investigating the causes of that beauty which pleases the eyes and which has the force to surprise our heart by the sweetness of its impressions upon us. . . . Because of the fear of allowing some prejudice to blind me, my first concern has been to treat my subject without paying attention to anyone else, no matter who it might be. I have tried to forget that I have seen human beings, that I have read books; I have distanced from my mind all the impressions that I had received in order to withdraw into myself and to reduce my ideas to the most simple and indubitable notions.[3]

Crousaz was the first philosopher in France to attempt to apply Cartesian rigor to aesthetics. He tells us[4] that he will carefully avoid building on doubtful principles and that

> I shall conduct myself with all the order and precaution possible. I shall not pass to a second thought without

having well established the preceding one, and I prefer even to invest my discourse with a few superfluous reflections than to hazard a few specious truths and to let a few of my propositions rest half-proved.[5]

Like Locke, Crousaz mentions the occasion which gave birth to his essay, and, at the same time, he deepens his commitment to the Cartesian method:

A conversation concerning the beauty of a palace was the occasion of this work. In order to establish more nicely what one should think about this subject, one thought that it would be necessary to go back to first principles, to the nature of beauty itself.[6]

Although he adds in the same dedication that "in order to deduce from true principles the reasons why one attributes certain beauties to music, a long digression on physics has been necessary," I shall avoid his antiquated, and sometimes quaint, notions on acoustics; that he thought it necessary to complement his philosophy with various experimental hypotheses reveals once again his commitment to Cartesianism. What is of chief interest is the way in which Crousaz deals with beauty and the Cartesian dichotomy between reason and sentiment.[7]

To discover what one means by calling something "beautiful," Crousaz asserts that one must introspect. Accordingly, one discovers that to say: " 'That is beautiful' . . . marks a certain rapport between an object and agreeable sensations, or with ideas of approbation. 'That is beautiful' is to say 'I apprehend something of which I approve, or something which gives me pleasure'."[8]

At this point in his argument Crousaz accepts the Cartesian dichotomy between reason and sentiment but vacillates in assigning beauty to one side or the other. He evidently wants to avoid drawing the same conclusions about beauty that

Descartes had drawn, that is, that our ideas of the beautiful are unstable, confused, unreliable, and represent no true quality of objects exterior to us. To avoid the same conclusion Crousaz begins by changing the premises.

According to Crousaz the self is a collection of perceptions, some of which he calls "ideas," others "sentiments." When, for example, he thinks of a circle, of a triangle, of a bird, of a house, so he tells us, he is forming "ideas." But when he is eating, when he is near a fire, or when he has a certain taste, then he has a "sentiment." But Crousaz is not satisfied with an ostensive definition of the two terms; he attempts a verbal definition: "Ideas occupy the mind while sentiments interest the heart. . . . Ideas amuse us, they exert our attention accordingly as they are more or less composite, more or less linked together."[9] Sentiments, however, "dominate us, take us over, . . . make us happy or unhappy. . . . One readily expresses one's ideas, but it is very difficult to describe one's sentiments."[10] We are masters of our ideas but not of our sentiments, which depend upon objects exterior to us. Ideas are said to be clear and distinct or not, either composed or simple; sentiments, however, are said to be weak or lively.

With these distinctions in hand and with the strong desire to make our knowledge of the beautiful as certain as our knowledge of mathematics, Crousaz proceeds to call our attention to a number of data which, he believes, prove the existence of a nonsentimental beauty: "Sometimes one recognizes that an object is very beautiful without being sensiby touched by it, and sometimes, on the contrary, one sees something with pleasure even though one does not find it beautiful, or barely beautiful."[11]

His first major conclusion is, therefore, that one has an idea of the beautiful which does not depend solely upon sentiment and which does not vary in accordance with the degree of pleasure derived from an object. Crousaz sees clearly that if one follows Descartes, "beauty" would be definable as "agreeable." He also sees that if this were true, one could establish a sort of calculus of the beautiful which would directly correspond to a calculus of pleasure. Crousaz does not deny that we often call something beautiful *and* are pleased and touched by it. But he points out, and rightly, that sometimes we recognize that an object is beautiful and that we believe for our own part that it is genuinely beautiful without our being pleased or touched; that is to say, we simply do not want to add "and it pleases me." It is as if a statement about our affective reaction to the object were inappropriate.

> One will say that this object has nothing which troubles him, or which gives him pleasure, though he recognizes it as beautiful. It is from this fact that one establishes the possibility of an object that is beautiful but that does not please, and consequently one does not correctly define "beautiful" by "that which pleases."[12]

The chief argument, then, that Crousaz finds in his own favor is the existence of a purely intellectual recognition of beauty. If this recognition exists, then Descartes is mistaken, and our ideas of the beautiful are to be assigned, at least in part, to the side of reason. Crousaz illustrates his argument by describing a certain man "who is considering something else, or whose heart is possessed by some violent passion, that is, if, for example, he is concerned about the result of a legal dispute. If such a man sees all the objects in the antechamber of the judge, whom he is impatiently waiting to see,"[13] he, Crousaz concludes, might readily recognize that the paintings on the walls are beautiful, that there are numerous handsome statues, without being touched by them at all. "There is, therefore, a beauty independent of sentiment, and our reason contains the speculative principles which teach us to decide, with sangfroid, whether an object is beautiful, or whether it is not."[14]

Just what these "speculative principles" are according to

Crousaz will be discussed in my next chapter; for the moment it is essential to see that he attempts to maintain the existence of a purely unaffective recognition of beauty. But it is all too easy to reply to his argument and to overturn his example. The most obvious objection is that the man he describes simply remembers having seen the objects when he was in a calm and untroubled state, and at that time they pleased him. One would readily grant that the pleasingness of an object is not a sufficient reason for calling it beautiful, but Crousaz wants to hold that pleasingness is not even a necessary condition. To state the matter more clearly, Crousaz wants to hold that not only is pleasingness not necessary, but that no affective or sentimental reaction of any kind is required. We shall see in a few moments, however, the way in which he will modify his position, and how he will struggle to maintain a sharp dichotomy between reason and sentiment and attempt to establish the rationality of beauty.

Another objection to his example is equally obvious. One might say that the man who simply recognizes the beauty of an object without being in any sense touched or moved is playing a game. One of the rules of certain societies is to make approving noises when one is faced with certain kinds of objects, that is, works of art. Some persons are actually pleased or touched by certain of these objects, and they make the noises. But the man that Crousaz describes is not touched at all, though he recognizes that these are the kinds of things that generally elicit noises of approval. And so, to avoid the censure of boorishness or crankiness, he plays the game.

Again, one might object that the man's recognition is an elliptical prediction; on the basis of his past experience, he is sure that if he were not so pressed and preoccupied he would be pleased by the object. But so much for objections to Crousaz's example. His conclusion is correct: one would not want to define the beautiful solely in terms of the agreeable, as Descartes implies. However, the argument that Crousaz gives

11

for his conclusion is not persuasive. Let us see how he tries to develop the theme of the rationality of beauty.

He asserts that he is looking for that idea which everyone has of the beautiful, but, because of the various sentiments that accompany it, it is often confused and not clearly distinguishable. He assumes that the idea is relative but in a specially restricted sense.

> When one asks what the beautiful is, one does not want to speak of an object which exists outside of us and is separated from all other objects, as when one asks what is a horse or a tree. . . . It is not so with beauty, for this term is not absolute but expresses the relation between objects, which we call "beautiful," and our ideas, or our sentiments, with our powers of apprehension or with our heart.[15]

According to Crousaz, beauty is not the only relative notion; propositional truth and moral rectitude are also relative in the sense defined as follows:

> A proposition is true by the relation that it bears to other propositions, or by the relation that it bears to the objects to which it [the proposition] is applied. The triangle has three angles, wood is inflammable. . . . We assert that an action is just by its conformity with our ideas of rectitude.[16]

The first weakening of the thesis that beauty is sometimes recognized by pure reason occurs so innocently, and with such ingenuousness, that one might overlook it. Crousaz asserts that it might occur "that one discovers something worthy of one's approbation, and which contains those traits which one could not help but esteem. Such an object pleases, and it does not please; it pleases the mind but not the sentiment."[17] He presents us with two sorts of beauty—that which pleases the reason and that which pleases the sentiment. There may be discords between the two as well as agreements: "Sometimes the ideas and the sentiments are in accord, and an object merits the name of beauty in a double sense; sometimes, on the contrary, the ideas and the sentiments combat one another."[18]

One would agree with Crousaz that there are "beauties that please the mind," for example, a good move in chess or an elegant proof in geometry, and one would agree that there are things which chiefly please one's sentiments, for example, love and gratitude. But it is obvious that after he has defined "reason" and "sentiment" as he has, we can accept his notion of "intellectual pleasures" only at the price of self-contradiction. For if pleasure and agreeableness belong to the passive side of our nature, and, if they overcome or dominate us, then to speak of a beauty pleasing the mind would be contradictory. The mind was described as active and as apprehending, the sentiments were said to be passive and simply occurring. Given Crousaz's assumptions, the mind might very well apprehend that the sentiments are pleased by an object, but that would be tantamount to reespousing Cartesianism, which is exactly what Crousaz attempts to avoid.

It is often the case, however, that the difficulties which appear to the critic appear to the author as well. Crousaz was apparently aware of the untenability of his position and almost entirely gives up Descartes for Malebranche:

> The body is incapable of acting by itself upon the soul, for what influence could extension possibly have on thought? If, therefore, certain sentiments regularly accompany certain movements, if the one agitates in the soul at the same time that the other agitates in the body, this consequence is the effect of an arbitrary coordination by the Author of Nature. His infinite intelligence . . . knows all the movements of which the human body,

His work, is susceptible, and at each moment He has assigned the sentiment which should accompany it. It is an economy which He established in creating man and even before He created him.[19]

To avoid the difficulties which the notion of intellectual beauties entail for Cartesianism, Crousaz tries to enlist the aid of a preestablished harmony and an aesthetic version of occasionalism:

This harmony between the nature of sentiments and the nature of objects which are the cause or occasion of such sentiments would have been perfectly constant and regular and would have been universal and without exception, if man had kept himself in that state in which his Creator placed him. But the Fall of Man and the consequences of the Fall . . . have doubtless greatly changed the constitution of human nature.[20]

Such is Crousaz's final statement concerning the relation between beauty, and reason and sentiment. First, he wants to hold that there are principles of aesthetic value which are known by the mind unaided by sentiment; he appears to believe that this proposition is essential in order to explain the universality and nonarbitrariness of the *bon goût*. We shall trace what he has to say about the *bon goût* in chapter 2. Secondly, he maintains that reason and sentiment are essentially different. Thirdly, he seeks refuge in an aesthetic occasionalism; at the moment when a certain person apprehends intellectually the beauty of an object, God has so foreordained things that the person feels certain sentiments of pleasure or agreeableness. And fourthly, recognizing that taste varies greatly from one man to another, from one civilization to another, he snatches at the doctrine of the Fall of Man. Doubtless Crousaz places too much strain upon one's imagination and credulity.

14

There were some aestheticians in France during the eighteenth century who did not feel as strongly about the tension between the Cartesian dichotomy of reason and sentiment, and who consequently did not indulge in the philosophical intricacies of such writers as Crousaz. J. B. Dubos, whose *Réflexions Critiques sur la poésie, la peinture et la musique* appeared in 1719, was a man of good sense but little sophistication. When he senses a philosophical difficulty, he is inclined to shrug, to be cavalier, or to change the subject.

His method is decidedly non-Cartesian, and his writings tend to be so loose that one is tempted to say he has no method at all. He has few general theories; he tends to be a sensualist: "I repeat, people give much greater credence to those who say to them 'I have seen' than to those who tell them 'I have concluded'."[21]

It is sentiment and only sentiment that informs us of the beauty of an object. Reason might give explanations or critiques, but it is neither necessary nor sufficient for our appreciation. "Since the chief end of poetry and painting is to touch us, poems and paintings are good only in proportion to their power to move and engage us."[22] He adds, "For sentiment teaches much better whether a work touches and whether it makes an impression upon us than all the dissertations composed by the critics to explain the merit and calculate the perfections and faults of a work."[23]

He admits that the means of discussion and analysis are effective when it is a question of explaining why a work pleases or not. It is sentiment that dictates whether an object is worthy to please.

> The work pleases or does it not? The work is good or
> bad in general? It is the same thing. Reasoning,
> therefore, should not interfere in the judgement that we
> bring to bear on a poem or on a painting except to
> explain the decision of sentiment and to show what faults

keep the object from pleasing or the beauties that make the object engaging.[24]

Like many of his contemporaries in England and in Germany, Dubos tries to profit from the banal comparison between the taste of the palate and aesthetic taste. "One tastes a ragout and even without knowing the rules one recognizes that it is good."[25] But he adds that the parallel is *en quelque manière* and feels obliged to widen the notion of sensation to include a "sixth sense."

> It is this sixth sense which is in us without our seeing
> its organs. It is that part of ourselves which judges
> on the impression which it feels and which, to make
> use of the terms of Plato [Republic 1. X] pronounces
> without consulting the rule and compass.[26]

According to Dubos, the heart is the organ, or the seat of the organ, of the sixth sense. It operates by itself and does not call upon reason for counsel or aid. When the right sort of object is presented to it, the sixth sense acts spontaneously. Speaking of the general public, he says:

> But as soon as the movements of their hearts, which
> operate mechanically, come to express themselves by a
> gesture, a certain countenance, those movements become
> a touchstone for knowing whether the object presented
> to them has or has not a certain merit.[27]

Although Dubos has a number of interesting observations to make in regard to rules, I shall put off this discussion until the next chapter.[28] As we have seen, what he has to say about the various roles of reason and sentiment is of no great moment; it represents the same opinion frequently encountered among his contemporaries. He confesses that some persons

16

have better taste than others, that one's sensibility to beauty sharpens upon exercising one's powers of observation. But instead of giving up the dualism of reason and sentiment, he merely asserts that there are two species of beauty, both of which are purely affective. The one is accessible to everyone who has the sixth sense—and according to Dubos this sense is almost universal—and the other is accessible to those of refined culture. But how it is possible that analysis and discrimination can alter one's sensibility—given the radical difference between reason and sentiment which Dubos accepts as a matter of course—is not explained.

If we take one of his comparisons seriously, we shall be forced to conclude that for Dubos an aesthetic judgement is either an exclamation like "Alas!" or "Great!" or a purely descriptive statement about one's personal feelings.

> When it is a question of judging the general effect of a
> work, the painter and the poet have as little right to
> reject those who do not know their art as a surgeon
> would have the right to reject the testimony of someone
> who has undergone an operation, when it is solely a
> question of knowing whether the operation was painful,
> under the pretext that the patient was ignorant of
> anatomy.[29]

According to Dubos, then, aesthetic judgements take the form of personal descriptions of affective states: "This work gave me a lot of pleasure." "This song depresses me." "This novel excites me." But of all the statements that one can make about works of art, these are surely the dullest and least informative.

Trublet takes issue with Dubos on many points, and, though remaining faithful to the Cartesian dualism of reason and sentiment, he tries to give a more exacting and sensitive account of aesthetic experience. In his *Essais sur divers sujets de littérature et de morale,* the first two volumes of which were published in Amsterdam in 1735, Trublet begins, naturally enough for the period, by asking whether one should judge works of art, or as he says *ouvrages de l'esprit,* by discussion or sentiment. "Moreover one must admit a great difference between feeling and understanding."[30] But Trublet drifts so far away from orthodox Cartesianism that sentiments become not only simple and composite but also clear and distinct.

Trublet's first complaint against Dubos centers upon the tired comparison of the palate's taste with aesthetic taste:

> It is not exactly the same sort of thing with spiritual taste as with physical or with a good work of the mind as with a good ragout, and certainly one sometimes abuses the comparison. If I do not find a ragout good, all that one can tell me will not help me to find it better. But what one will tell me about a beautiful work can often greatly contribute to making me feel the beauty. Intellectual taste is susceptible of instruction, while physical taste is not.[31]

The difference between the two is immense, as Trublet notes. One does not censure someone who disagrees with us about physical taste, though one often does so when it is a question of intellectual or aesthetic taste. Again, there is next to nothing that one can say to help someone appreciate an object of physical taste, though with aesthetic taste one can instruct, illuminate, and analyze. Also, with physical taste there is no question of exactitude or truth. But as Trublet points out, in paintings and in novels one often demands verisimilitude and accuracy, even if of an oblique or distant sort. To the degree that a certain work of art is representative, the notions of truth and precision become relevant to the responses of sentiment. But physical taste bears no relation to objects beyond itself; one has the sensation of sweetness or of bitterness but nothing more.

If, so Trublet argues, the notions of truth and exactitude, as well as the rules, are necessary in determining the worth of an object of art, then argument and discussion are essential not only to explain why one has certain sentiments about a work of art but also to make the sentiments possible. A person who had only sentiments would be like a scientist who had only senses; he could only amass a confused series of affective experiences, leading nowhere, and having no definite character.

> One will tell me, perhaps, that there are great beauties
> which make themselves felt to everyone; for example,
> those that one calls particularly the beauties of sentiment.
> I reply first that, although everybody feels certain beau-
> ties, not everybody feels them equally. Secondly, there
> are a great many beauties, and some of them the highest,
> which are only felt by persons of great intellectual
> accomplishment. As for the sentiments, they are
> accessible to everybody only when they are simple and
> simply expressed. If they are a bit composite, or
> rendered with finesse and elegance, they escape the
> multitude, and sometimes they even appear to them to
> be false.[32]

One naturally thinks of Marivaux, one of the most elegant and sensitive writers of the eighteenth century, whose works appeared to some of his contemporaries, and to many of the later generation, as "false." "Marivaudage" became synono-mous with "false and affected subtility of sentiment." It is only to be expected that a man like Voltaire would write so harshly against him.

In Trublet one can trace the gradual narrowing of the gap between sentiment and reason. He asks the reader to imagine a nation composed of persons so intellectually superior to our-selves that the least endowed of them would greatly surpass the most endowed among ourselves. "Our critics would con-fess that there was at least a great deal of *esprit* in their works;

but they would not find any taste. These people, our critics would say, write only enigmas."[33]

Trublet, an ardent believer in the aristocracy of taste, was the first French aesthetician to describe a peculiarly aesthetic sensibility. He accepted the bifurcation of the soul into the various sorts of cogitation on the one hand and feelings and emotions on the other. But he wanted to show that there is another, autonomous, realm, which is neither cerebral nor visceral. The weight of the Cartesian dichotomy, however, proved to be too heavy. In none of his writings does he attempt an analysis of the peculiarly aesthetic sensibility; he contents himself with such vague suggestions as the following:

> I admit that this sort of reader [he is speaking of the ordinary and mildly educated reader] can feel a great part of their beauties; but one would deceive oneself greatly to believe that they are in the state to feel all of them or in all their breadth. I say not only that they could not explain these beauties, but that they could not even feel them.[34]

A few aestheticians of the period tried to explain aesthetic reactions in a purely mechanistic manner. Pierre Estève, for example, in *L'Esprit des beaux-arts* (1753) accepts without hesitation the orthodoxy of the century, that sentiment and reason are essentially different, and describes aesthetic response without any reference to the intellect. It is as though one's beliefs, intellectual commitments, and semirational penchants—which Trublet had tried to relate to aesthetic feeling—did not exist:

> One can notice, first af all, that all the sentiments which make the fine arts felt begin with the emotions of the organs or, rather, with sensations. The movements of the nerves carry to the soul an intense clarity which makes the soul judge and approve, but, because the

emotions of the senses are here what is essential, the
pure pleasure of the movements of the organ will be the
principle that is capable of sustaining the constant
perfections in the fine arts. This involuntary instinct
which is called "taste" and which decides what is beautiful has its origin in the mechanical pleasure of the senses.
It is thus that without the help of a slow reflection
(which is also often unsure) one feels oneself penetrated
by the truth of emotion. The simple movements of the
organ will produce an agreeable affection . . . and one will
be preserved from having recourse to ingenious justi-
fications and sublime subtilities.[35]

Estève holds that a science of aesthetics is possible, but
that it must be founded on mechanistic principles. The mind
would take notice of the modifications of the body and, by at-
tending to the various emotions produced by certain objects of
art, would formulate certain principles. Consequently, criticism
would be a branch of either anatomy or physiology.

Although the true science of sensibility has its principles
in the mechanism of the sensations, one should not
conclude that the mind cannot give any precepts; far from
it. It is exactly in making itself attentive to the effects
of the lively passions that it is capable of instructing
itself concerning the principles that move us.[36]

Although the stimulus of Cartesianism was of great importance to mathematics and physics during the eighteenth century, it cannot be doubted that Cartesianism greatly retarded
aesthetic philosophy and often turned the subject into something that it is not—a variety of applied physics or medicine
or psychology. One has little hope for a writer like Charles
Bonnet who introduces his few observations on aesthetics by
an immense and resounding Cartesian-Malebranchian credo. In

his *Essai Analytique,* dedicated to Frederick V of Denmark and Norway, he states:

> I suppose that man is a composite of two substances,
> one immaterial, the other corporeal. One expresses that
> in two words when one says that man is a mixed being . . .
> this "I" which perceives, which compares, which reasons,
> this "I" which has the notions of extension, division,
> movement, etc., this "I" which modifies itself in so many
> different ways, is always simple, indivisible. . . . I suppose
> that the body acts upon the soul, or, if one prefers,
> that on the occasion of the movements that objects excite
> in the senses, the activity of the soul deploys itself in a
> certain manner, from which are born the sensations and
> volitions. . . . I assume, then, that the union of the soul
> and the body and their reciprocal influence is a phenome-
> non whose laws I can study. . . . I confess that I do not
> understand how an idea can be the cause of a move-
> ment, or how a movement can be the cause of an idea.
> . . . The idea that I have of body differs essentially
> from that which I have of soul.[37]

Given so many philosophical inhibitions, an author such as Bonnet could do little more than produce the various permutations of his axioms.

With Batteux, in his *Les Beaux-Arts réduits à un même principe* (1747), we encounter not only a man more sensitive to the fine arts than such writers as Bonnet and Estève but also less doctrinaire and less given to the philosophical orthodoxies of the day. His work had considerable influence in France during the eighteenth century and also during the nineteenth. Although he begins by radically separating reason from sentiment, he is driven, during the course of his work, to asserting that they are in some way, given certain conditions, almost identical.

To distinguish the applied from the fine arts, Batteux invokes pleasure. The fine arts are born "from joy and the sentiments which produce abundance and tranquility."[38] The applied arts are purely utilitarian. There is a third species, which combines utility and pleasure, for example, eloquence and architecture. Batteux tells the reader straight away, "We are going to speak here only about the fine arts, that is to say, those which have as their chief object, pleasure."[39] But he quickly adds that these pleasures must be either auditory or visual. The arts are, therefore, divided into music and poetry on the one side, and painting and architecture on the other. Just what the *même principe* is that Batteux believes he has discovered, I shall explain in the next chapter. Let us now examine the way in which he deals with reason and sentiment. "Intelligence considers what objects are in themselves, according to their essence, without any relation to ourselves. Taste, on the contrary, occupies itself solely with objects as they are related to ourselves."[40]

One would be inclined to object that this definition is too wide, for we speak about many things and their relation to ourselves without meaning to speak about taste: optical illusions, odors, and objects in perspective. The fault is not remedied by what follows: "And so I define intelligence as the faculty of knowing the true and the false and of distinguishing them one from the other. And taste is the faculty of feeling the good, the bad, the mediocre, and distinguishing them with certainty."[41]

One is inclined to object that if taste were in need of defining, one is not greatly advanced by being introduced to the good, the bad, and the mediocre. Moreover, it appears that taste has at least some relation to the beautiful, but in his definition Batteux speaks only of the good. He tells us that

> our soul knows, and what it knows produces in it a
> sentiment. Knowledge is a light spread throughout our

23

soul; sentiment is a movement which agitates. The one
illuminates, the other heats. The one makes us see
an object, the other draws us to it or turns us from it.
. . . Taste is therefore a sentiment.[42]

It appears that aesthetic values are confounded with ethical. Batteux tells us that taste is to the fine arts what intelligence is to the sciences. Their objects are different, but their
functions have a considerable analogy. He assumes that both
reason and sentiment apprehend: intelligence *knows*, while taste
feels the good. Taste is a kind of sentiment and has for its
object works of art.

Aesthetic sentiment is not unrelated, so Batteux maintains,
to *lumière* or to *un éclair de lumière*. His description of the
"mechanism" of aesthetic reaction is both complicated and contradictory. It is complicated in that he tries to maintain a
hybrid of sentiment and reason. A bolt of *lumière* precedes
sentiment, "brusquely," as he says, and so quickly that the
mind cannot apprehend or perceive it. "But this operation is
so rapid that often one is not even aware of it, and the reason,
when it returns upon the sentiment, has a great deal of difficulty in recognizing the cause."[43] His description is contradictory because he has already defined the terms "sentiment"
and "reason" so that a *tertium quid* that links the two, partaking of the properties of both, would be logically impossible. He
tries to argue that, though the two are distinct, *lumière* suddenly apprehends the beauty of an object and is immediately
followed by a sentimental response. The entire process is so
quick that the mind is left not quite knowing what has hap-
pened. But though this sort of prestidigitation amuses au-
diences, it does not solve philosophical problems. For clearly
lumière and *éclair de lumière*, given Batteux's dualism, cannot
be other than a special application of reason.

Although this sentiment appears to depart brusquely
and blindly, it is, however, always preceded by at least

an *éclair de lumière*, by virtue of which we discover the
qualities of the object. It is necessary that the chord
be struck before the sound is heard.[44]

If one is to interpret this last metaphor, it seems that the
mind first apprehends the beauty of an object, and, afterward,
the feeling of pleasure occurs.

Batteux has several reasons for wanting to hold to the
temporal priority of reason in matters of taste. First, when
dealing with rules and standards of taste, Batteux will attempt
to argue that there is only one correct taste, and this is dictated
by nature. I shall put off that discussion until the next chapter.
Secondly, he holds that one of the chief purposes of the fine
arts is to satisfy one's *amour propre*. If that is so, then reason
should be a better judge of what is to one's own interest than
sentiment. The emotions are often mendacious, capricious,
vague, and not to one's own true interest. In the fine arts one
is presented with objects that have an intimate relation with
ourselves, for they imitate the better aspects of human life and
society, as well as the nobler and purer regions of nature.
Thirdly, given his theory of imitation and *la belle nature*—
which I shall defer until the third chapter—Batteux would have
to maintain, if he is to be consistent, that reason instead of
sentiment apprehends beauty. He holds that the fine arts are
essentially imitative of *la belle nature*, and that they have as
one of their ends the representation of nature's elegance, simplicity, unity, variety, and proportion. To decide whether
something is a good imitation is evidently a matter for judgement, not for sentiment. But though his reasons for holding
his doctrine of the brusque *éclair de lumière* might be tenable,
one wonders what importance the sentiments have in aesthetic
reactions.

He attempts to reply by saying:

But what good would it do us to know if we did not
enjoy? Nature was too wise not to separate these two

parts, and, in giving us the faculty of knowing, she could not refuse that of feeling—the relation of the object known with its usefulness to us—and to be drawn to it by sentiment. It is sentiment that one calls natural taste because it is nature which has given it to us.[45]

Batteux, in effect, tries to present us with another way of reconciling sentiment and reason, though the terms are logically irreconcilable in the context of his system. When the reason meditates about a certain object and begins to arrive at a clear understanding of it, a kind of natural heat and intensity develops within the understanding; then, given the affinity of intellectual fervor with the warmth of the sentiments, taste and aesthetic appreciation occur spontaneously. It is as if the mind were brimming over with intellectual excitement, and the sentiments —like the basin of a fountain—caught the froth of the superfluous waters. The result, according to Batteux, is aesthetic appreciation or taste.

The objections to this description are so obvious that one hesitates to mention them. One sees that Batteux has put himself in the same embarrassing position as Descartes. Just as the pineal gland was the seat of the interaction of the body and the soul, so, according to Batteux, a certain degree of intellectual intensity binds the reason with sentiment.

In a further attempt to reconcile the two parts of human nature, Batteux wanders even more deeply into the jungles of contradiction. He tells us, "Taste is an understanding of the rules by means of the sentiment."[46] But he has already told us that one understands by means of the reason and feels by means of taste. Furthermore, science belongs to the understanding, while the fine arts belong to aesthetic sentiment or taste. Contradictions become even more luxuriant in the passage that follows:

For objects to please our mind it suffices that they be perfect in themselves. The mind considers them disinterestedly, and, provided that it finds regularity, boldness of conception and elegance, it is satisfied. However, it is a different matter with the heart. It is touched by objects only in so far as they are to its own interest. It is that which determines its love or its hatred.[47]

Given the other propositions of his system, one would naturally infer that Batteux is drawing a distinction between science and art. But though consistency would have it so, Batteux will not:

From this it follows that the mind ought to be more satisfied with works of art which present the beautiful than with the objects of nature, which almost always have some imperfection, and that the heart, on the contrary, should be less interested in artificial objects than in natural objects because it has less advantage to expect something from artificial objects.[48]

It now appears that only reason is the judge of the fine arts; it knows the rules and applies them to particular objects presented to it. Accordingly, the fine arts become a branch of science. Just as a botanist or zoologist might take pleasure in finding a perfect or almost perfect specimen of a certain species of plant or animal, so, too, the man of taste takes pleasure in finding objects that conform as closely as possible to the rules. Aesthetic appreciation would then resemble the glee of the taxidermist or butterfly collector. We shall see in the next chapter, however, that Batteux recants a great many of the consequences of his system. Even on general grounds this should not be surprising, for the title of his treatise on aesthetics, *The Fine Arts Reduced to a Single Principle,* is enough to make even a novice a little suspicious.

In 1741 a book appeared on the fine arts which hardly startled Paris, and which, therefore, barely made its way across the frontiers of France. Nonetheless, it contained the central thesis, or at least one of the central theses, of a book which has had great influence on twentieth-century aestheticians and ethicists: G. E. Moore's *Principia Ethica.* In Father André's modest volume entitled *Essai sur le beau,* one is introduced to aesthetics with the customary grace and elegance of eighteenth-century French essayists. One soon realizes that the author is both Cartesian and Malbranchian, like many of the other writers whom we have so far encountered.

> The work that one is presenting to the public owes its birth to a dispute that arose among certain men of letters concerning the beautiful. Each of them was reasoning in a rather carefree manner without proposing the principles upon which it would be necessary to agree in order to think correctly. One of those who had taken part in the dispute proposed to himself to establish principles which would be both certain and indubitable.[49]

This good man was, of course, Père André. He agreed with the principal writers of the period that there exists a connection between aesthetic beauty and pleasure. But according to André the connection is not simply one of fact; it is not the case that, if something pleases, it, therefore, has aesthetic value. He adamantly denies that aesthetic value can be defined in terms of "pleasurableness." André formulated G. E. Moore's naturalistic fallacy perhaps with less vigor but certainly with less truculence:

> I call something "beautiful" in a work of the spirit not that which pleases at the first glance of the imagination . . . but, rather, that which has the right to please—the right to please both the powers of reason and of reflection by the excellence of the object, by its own light and correctness, and, if one allows me the term, by its intrinsic worth.[50]

28

Unlike Dubos and certain other writers of the period, André observes that the question "But is the object that *does* please me *worthy* of pleasing me?" is legitimate. In regard to the dispute between reason and sentiment, André swears allegiance to the former. Although he holds nothing against enjoying works of art—as so many artists of the twentieth century do—André maintains that intellectual discrimination ought to precede enjoyment. Since he puts his point so charmingly himself, there is no reason not to quote it:

> Here, Sirs, I seem to hear certain murmurs among our philosophers, "Is it, therefore, that we are going to abandon grace [of style] to the charge of two blind persons—to the imagination which is a mad woman and to the heart which is an imbecile, always a slave either to its furies or to its weaknesses?"[51]

André answers, as one would expect from his definition of beautiful, "No." The mind, by its own powers or more specifically, by the principles which André believes he has discovered, acts as a control over the imagination and as a calmative to the heart. André was not the first of the aestheticians of the Enlightenment to note the difficulties in purely naturalistic or factual definitions of aesthetic value or of beauty, for Crousaz had already written:

> Good taste makes us first esteem by sentiment what the reason would have approved of after it had given itself the time to examine the matter closely and to form correct ideas of the object. Bad taste, on the contrary, makes us feel with pleasure what the reason would not have approved of.[52]

André was the first writer to contest such theories as those of Dubos, who attempted to define aesthetic values in purely psychological terms. As we have noted, Dubos tried to maintain a number of incompatible theories at the same time. But the theory which appears to have been the most offensive to André was Dubos's theory of therapeutic art. This, of course, is not Dubos's term, but it characterizes his thought. Dubos had maintained that all pleasures occur from the satisfaction of a certain need, and that the intensity of the satisfaction depends upon the ardor of the need. Dubos had maintained, secondly, that the body and the sentiments have their cravings, just as the soul has its longings and requirements. The most pressing need of the soul is to be occupied. Nothing is more insupportable than inactivity, for then the soul turns in upon itself, feeds upon itself, languishes, perhaps gives birth to sick or monstrous speculations, and finishes by stultifying itself:

> One of the greatest needs of man is to have his mind occupied. Ennui, which soon follows the inaction of the soul, is such a painful affliction for man that he often undertakes the most arduous work in order to free himself from the pain of being tormented by ennui.[53]

At this point Dubos introduces his theory, or rather one of his several theories, concerning the nature of aesthetic value. Art is a kind of game which liberates the mind from ennui. However interesting Dubos's theory might be—and I shall examine it in chapter 4—one can readily see why such writers as Father André would have had some reservations about it. André would not have denied that boredom is insupportable, and, surely, given his profession, he was not unacquainted with it. But André would object that if one defines aesthetic value in purely psychological terms, then the question of the worthiness of satisfactions could not arise. The most one could say is that a given work of art satisfies a certain person's needs more than another work. Though one might try to extend the theory by a sort of aesthetic calculus, i.e., by employing the notions of duration, purity, universality, propinquity, and the intensity of the pleasure, Father André's question would still be legitimate, "But is the object *worthy* of our aesthetic appreciation?"[54] Unfortunately, however, as it is so often with the writers with whom we are dealing, André does not develop his point but moves on quickly to another.

Several minor writers of the period simply announce their allegiance to one or the other of the two camps of reason and sentiment without engaging in any of the artifice of such writers as Crousaz. The Marquis d'Argens, for example, in his *Réflexions Historiques et critiques sur le goût et sur les ouvrages des principaux auteurs anciens et modernes* (1743) says:

> Those who consider taste to be something arbitrary and
> almost capricious do not rightly consider the matter.
> Taste is something objectively existant. . . . I define taste
> as a natural sentiment, perfected and enlightened by
> a perfect understanding of everything which makes
> objects brilliant, precise, profound, or elegant.[55]

Louis de Jaucourt, writing for the *Encyclopédie*, had nothing but confusion to add to the discussion between reason and sentiment:

> Considered as faculties, good taste and good sense are
> only a single thing; good sense is a certain rectitude of
> the soul which sees the true and the just and is attracted
> to it. Good taste is the same rectitude by which the
> soul sees the good and approves of it. The difference
> between the two is discovered in regard to their objects.
> Good sense is ordinarily confined to things that are
> sensible, while good taste to more refined and elevated
> objects. Thus good taste, conceived of in this way,
> is nothing but good sense refined and directed towards
> delicate and elevated objects. Good sense is nothing

but good taste limited to more sensible and material
objects. The true is the object of taste as well as the
good, and the mind has its taste as well as the heart.[56]

Charles Rollin asserts the same point of view in his *De la
manière d'enseigner et d'étudier les belles-lettres* (1726–1728).
Taste is "this happy quality which one feels better than one is
able to define, and which is less the effect of genius than of
judgement; it is a species of natural reason perfected by
study."[57] Once again one finds an attempt to invent a faculty
which is neither reason nor sentiment but somehow both at the
same time.

Roger de Piles, in his *Diverses Conversations sur la peinture* (1777), wants to make short work of his philosophy so
that he can quickly turn to his true interest, painting: "I shall
simply say to you that, generally speaking, taste, in matters of
the mind, is nothing other than the manner in which the mind
is capable of envisaging things according to whether it is well
or badly formed; that is to say, accordingly as it has conceived
a good or bad idea of them. Good taste in a work of art is a
conformity of the parts with the whole and the whole with perfection."[58] Once again it appears that reason discovers whether
something satisfies the requirements of the archetype, and afterward sentiment, like an enthusiastic audience, applauds the discovery that reason has made.

It should be noted that some writers on taste eschewed the
Cartesian dichotomy between reason and sentiment, but they
did so not because they thought it was untenable, but, rather,
because their interests in philosophy were slender. Consequently, one often encounters such cavalier descriptions of taste
as the following:

In a word the most necessary quality, not only for the
art of conversation but for the entire conduct of life and

> for the sciences, is this taste, this prudence, this discern-
> ment, which teaches in regard to every matter and on
> every occasion what must be done and how it must
> be done.[59]

Taste becomes so broad that it encompasses all human activities—the arts, the sciences, and the interactions of mankind in
society. But though it is true that during the Regency the notions of *bon goût* and correctness dominated all aspects of life
among the aristocracy, one wonders how the same *bon goût*
could teach one how to reason in the sciences, how to comport
oneself with other human beings, and how to appreciate the
fine arts.

When one thinks of the principal philosophers of the
French Enlightenment, one naturally remembers the names of
Voltaire, d'Alembert, Montesquieu, Condillac, Diderot, and
Rousseau. The reader might ask why I have not yet mentioned
them. Rousseau, however, was a man who felt strongly about
a great many things, but who thought clearly about almost
nothing. Though I should not like to make short work of such
an influential figure, I believe that the distinction mentioned
earlier between critical and aesthetic theories allows me to do
so. Rousseau's enthusiasm about nature, vertiginous heights,
boundless lakes, long walks in the countryside, human sentiments—all this is well known. But in none of his writings does
he address himself to the philosophical questions which concerned so many of the writers whom we have met. He will
appear, however, in the last chapter of this work, where we
shall examine the relationships between art and morality.

As for Condillac, though we shall discover an interesting
theory of the genesis and role of the fine arts in his works, the
problem of reason and sentiment seems not to have interested
him. This is unfortunate, because he was a man of considerable philosophical acumen.

Diderot's complicated and contradictory way of dealing with the problem will be examined at the end of the present chapter.

It is natural to deal with Voltaire, d'Alembert, and Montesquieu together in regard to the problem under study because an elegant volume, *Essai sur le goût*, appeared in Paris in 1766 which contained an essay by each of these three philosophers. The book was compiled and given a tedious preface by Alexandre Gérard.

Voltaire's essay, also entitled "Essai sur le goût," is the least interesting of the three. Voltaire took many subjects lightly, but he came close to dismissing certain subjects entirely, and among them was aesthetics. Throughout his writings there are abundant critical theories and criticisms of work of art, for example, in his *Siècle de Louis XIV*. But what he has to say about the Cartesian dichotomy is too gallant and vague to be of much help:

> It follows, therefore, that taste in general is nothing other
> than a lively discernment, a prompt perception, which,
> in the same way as the sensation of the palate, anticipates
> reflection and makes us find in the good an exquisite and
> voluptuous pleasure and repulses us from the contrary
> with distaste.[60]

Sometimes Voltaire speaks as though beauty were independent of the mind and something discoverable; more frequently he describes taste as a kind of feeling which can be developed, heightened, and educated. It is interesting to note that he contrasts clear and distinct feelings with those that are confused and vague, in much the same way that Descartes had described ideas:

> True taste does not consist in a vague and confused sensation, but in a distinct vision, in a lively and reasoned

discernment of different qualities, according to the relation and the connections that these qualities have in the object that we contemplate.[61]

One needs time, instruction, and experience to form *le goût intellectuel*. *Le goût sensuel*, on the contrary, is brutish, unalterable, and confused. It would naturally follow from this distinction that the trite expression "There is no disputing about taste" is false, given one interpretation of taste, and true, given another:

One commonly says that there is no disputing about taste. This maxim is true if by "taste" one understands the palate which rejects certain forms of alimentation and likes others, because it is useless to dispute about things that cannot be changed, and because one cannot reform the constitution and mechanism of the bodily organs. But the maxim is both false and pernicious when one applies it to the intellectual taste, which has the arts and the sciences for object. Just as these objects have objectively existing blandishments, so, too, there is a good taste which truly perceives them, and a bad taste which does not.[62]

Voltaire adds that there do exist certain *esprits phlegmatiques* which become excited about nothing in the fine arts, and certain *esprits mal faits* which are irremediably limited. It would be pointless to speak to them about taste because they have none at all. However, if one takes Voltaire's distinction between sensual and intellectual taste seriously, and if the former are indocile and the latter tractable, and if, lastly, *le bon goût* is a form of intellectual taste, then surely Voltaire has contradicted himself. Though it would be pointless to ask a man who has no sense of smell to discriminate among certain odors, it would not be useless to try to help someone appreciate a certain work of art. Even if he were completely unacquainted with the fine arts he would still be teachable. One would have to begin at the beginning, as one does when teaching geometry. But if aesthetic taste is a form of reason, as Voltaire asserts, one would not simply throw up one's hands and say that the student is *phlegmatique* and intransigent. If the student were stupid, then, of course, one could not teach him much of anything. And if he had a certain penchant or interest, he might not be inclined to give much time to another subject. But faced with the obvious phenomenon of persons without any taste whatsoever, Voltaire tries to take refuge in a comparison between them and persons who are, for example, colorblind or tone-deaf. This comparison belies his assertion that aesthetic taste is a form of intelligence.

D'Alembert's essay is entitled "Réflexions sur l'usage et l'abus de la philosophie dans les matières de goût." With his customary clarity, d'Alembert lets the reader know immediately what his assumptions are: "Taste, though hardly common, is not arbitrary; this truth is recognized equally by those who reduce taste to feeling, and by those who limit it to reasoning."[63] He assumes, furthermore, that the purpose of philosophy, when directed toward the fine arts, is to analyze our pleasures and to discover in what the principles of pleasure consist.

> If taste is not arbitrary, then it is, therefore, founded on incontestable principles, and the necessary consequence of that proposition is: there should not exist any object of art which cannot be judged by applying these principles.[64]

According to d'Alembert, these principles are within us. He distinguishes between principles of physics and those of the fine arts. The former are outside of us and often extremely difficult to discover. When one reaches an impasse one says that one needs more data, or that certain of the assumptions must be changed. An impasse concerning a physical principle is a confession of temporary ignorance. The latter principles are within us, that is, they are mechanisms of our feelings and sensations. In matters of taste one does not speak about the object, so d'Alembert holds, but rather about its reactions upon our sensibility. When one reaches an impasse concerning aesthetic principles, one should simply say that nothing else can be said about the matter.

> We should dispense with forever mounting toward first
> principles, which for us are always behind a cloud.
> To want to find the metaphysical cause of our pleasures
> would be an undertaking as chimerical as trying to
> explain the action of an object upon our senses. . . . One
> can reduce the principles of our pleasures in matters
> of taste to a small number of incontestable observations
> concerning our way of feeling.[65]

Given one interpretation of this statement, d'Alembert is obviously in the right. If one explains why a certain novel pleased one by saying that its plot was intriguing or the characters lively and well drawn or the language rich and subtle, and then if one were asked, "But why do those characteristics please you?" one would be more inclined to laugh than to reply. There is nothing else to be said. But given another interpretation, the statement is false. D'Alembert often speaks as a psychologist and assimilates aesthetic criticism to psychological investigation. If the two were the same, then one might reach the same sort of impasse in psychology that one sometimes reaches in aesthetics.

In regard to the dualism that haunted so many writers of the period, d'Alembert's reply is both sensitive and tragic:

> One can, so it seems to me, in accordance with these
> reflections, reply in two words to the question, often

hotly entertained, of whether the sentiment is preferable
to discussion in judging a work of art. Sensation is the
natural judge at the first moment, and the discussion
is the judge afterward. With persons who join finesse
and promptitude with correctness of the mind, the second
judge will usually simply confirm the judgements of
the former. But, one will say, since they are not always
in accord, would it not be better in every case to give
heed to the first decision which sentiment pronounces?
. . . We reply with regret that such is the misfortune of
the human condition; we rarely acquire new knowledge
without having to disabuse ourselves of some agreeable
illusion, and our understanding is almost always at the
expense of our pleasures.[66]

As knowledge increases, so do desires and, therefore, needs.
Since the latter are restless and often unsatisfied, trouble and
anguish naturally arise.

D'Alembert is something of an aesthetic primitivist. In
the early days when man reflected upon very little, one could
enjoy profoundly the beauties of nature and art. Just as the
lover begins to see faults in the object of his love and to reflect
upon the lover's actions and motivations, so, too, the intellectual man begins to see the causes and mechanisms of his
pleasure. In the former case love might diminish, in the latter,
so d'Alembert holds, our pleasures pale and disappear.

Montesquieu's essay, or rather fragment of an essay, is
entitled "Essai sur le goût, dans les choses de la nature et de
l'art." As is well known, Montesquieu's interests lay elsewhere than in the fine arts, notably in political theory and
philosophy of history. But he has a few curious comments to
make on the dualism of mind and body, and aesthetic taste.

In our present manner of existence, our soul feels three
sorts of pleasures: there are those which it draws from

38

its own existence; others which result from its union with the body; and others which are found upon the bent and prejudices of certain institutions, of certain customs and habits.[67]

In the same essay, Montesquieu often refers to the body as "our machine." The machine is somehow related to the soul, which has an additional faculty, le goût. Taste is "nothing other than the advantage of discovering with finesse and promptitude the degree of pleasure that each thing ought to give to men."[68] He asserts that if the soul had not been united to the machine, it would, nonetheless, have had knowledge and would also have loved what it knew. Montesquieu appears to be describing a purely intellectual love in the Platonic tradition. "But at present we love almost always only that which we do not know."[69]

Upon the first reading, one has the impression that Montesquieu's distinction between the goût naturel and the goût acquis will correspond to the bodily machine on the one hand, and the soul on the other. He asserts that the goût naturel is not a knowledge of theory but, rather, a prompt and exact application of rules that one does not even know. He adds, "Thus what we can say here is that all the precepts that we could give for taste will regard only acquired taste."[70] But then we are quickly informed that the goût acquis indirectly influences, changes, augments, and diminishes the goût naturel, just as the goût naturel affects, changes, and augments the goût acquis. What Montesquieu has in mind is obviously true, for what might seem to be affected or unnatural art in one culture might be so customary that anything else would seem unnatural in another culture. Or again, the manners of the French aristocracy before the Revolution of 1789 might have appeared punctilious and formal to the peasantry. It is difficult, therefore, to say precisely what constitutes natural taste, or the natural man, without referring to a particular society during a particular period of time. That recurring theme in Western civilization—"return to nature"—is little more than a plea to adopt a new and different set of affectations.

Montesquieu is the only writer of the period who accepts the orthodox dualism of sentiment and reason, only to equate the two terms:

> Taste . . . is that which attaches us to an object by means of the sentiment, but this does not hinder its being able to attach itself to intellectual things, the knowledge of which gives so much pleasure to the soul that it was the only felicity of certain philosophers. The soul knows by means of its ideas and by means of its sentiments; for, although we oppose idea to sentiment, even so, when one sees a thing, one feels it, and there is nothing so intellectual that the soul sees or believes it sees, that it does not also feel.[71]

By way of refuting Montesquieu one might remember doing geometry when one was young: one did the problems mechanically, understanding them, but feeling nothing. Montesquieu cannot oppose the *goût naturel* to the *goût acquis* and then add that the soul knows by means of its ideas and its sentiments. Had he continued his analysis of aesthetic taste, Montesquieu might have been able to rid himself entirely of the antiquated Cartesian dualism, for we have seen how he strains under its weight.

I shall conclude the present chapter with an examination of Diderot's position concerning the roles of reason and sentiment. And I might as well be candid at the beginning instead of embarrassed at the conclusion. Although Diderot is always an interesting and stimulating writer, consistency was not one of his virtues. I do not mean to imply that he vaunted his contradictions and indulged in willful paradox, like certain philosophers of our own day, but rather with Diderot one encounters a philosopher who seems to have suffered from curious lapses of memory. Within the space of two paragraphs he often seems to have forgotten what he has already maintained. Whether this pernicious inconsistency of his writings is the result of his wide interests, or his volatile nature, or the haste with which he was compelled to write many of his works, I cannot say. But one would certainly not want to dismiss him by saying that he was a poor philosopher; for, though he never pursues an idea with the tenacity which one encounters, for example, in Hume, he offers the reader, and especially one who is interested in aesthetics, a richness of ideas that has few philosophical equals.

In his *Recherchés Philosophiques sur l'origine et la nature du beau*[72] which was the title of Naigeon in the *Oeuvres* of Diderot, published in 1798, and which first appeared in separate form in Amsterdam in 1772, Diderot, after a long disquisition about writers on aesthetics from Plato to Shaftesbury, asserts that *beau* is a term that applies to an infinity of objects. It must, nonetheless, have a single signification: "But whatever difference there might be among these objects, it must be the case that either we falsely apply the term *beau* or that there be among all these objects a single quality of which the term *beau* is a sign."[73] One might like to complain immediately that one applies many terms to a large set of objects without our knowing a single common quality. To use Wittgenstein's well-known example, we call a multitude of things "games" without being able to specify a single common quality: board games, field games, patience, charades, and so on. We could specify a number of properties which have a strong tendency to limit our applying "game" to various objects, but we could not name a common and peculiar property. But let us not belabor a point that has so frequently been made and simply observe at the outset that Diderot is looking, in the essay I have just mentioned, for a common and peculiar property which all things

41

called "beautiful" possess. His answer is that only the term "relationship" or the notion of *rapports* will do:

> For there is only the notion of relationships which is capable of these effects. . . . I call, therefore, something outside of me "beautiful" if it contains within itself that which will awaken in my understanding the idea of relationships, and I call something by relation to me "beautiful" everything which awakens this idea.[74]

Diderot had expressed this doctrine in earlier works, such as his *Mémoires de mathématiques*. But it is only in his essay on the *beau* that he attempts an analysis and justification of the doctrine. His first qualification is that only visible and audible qualities are to be included in the definition. His argument against including data from the so-called "lower sense organs" is purely linguistic; one does not speak of their data as beautiful. But we now encounter his first contradiction, for a few pages later in the same essay he tells us:

> It is the people that have made languages; it is up to the philosopher to discover the origin of objects, and it would hardly be surprising that the principles of the one should not often be in contradiction with the usages of the other.[75]

It might be that Diderot is right in excluding data from the lower senses. However, he cannot argue for their exclusion like a contemporary "ordinary language philosopher" and, at the same time, hold that linguistic forms do not count as evidence or counterevidence for a philosophical thesis. But let us move on to his theory concerning reason and sentiment.

Diderot asserts that one must distinguish between the forms which are in objects and the notion that one might have of them. "My understanding neither adds nor detracts anything from objects."[76]

> Whether I think or do not think of the façade of the
> Louvre, all the parts which compose it would not have
> less form or less arrangement among them; whether people
> exist or not, the façade would not be any the less beauti-
> ful but only for persons who are constituted like ourselves,
> that is, with a body and a mind; for, in regard to persons
> constituted otherwise, the façade would be neither
> beautiful nor ugly or even neither of the two.[77]

Diderot is, then, a kind of subjectivist. There exist certain objects which would be beautiful to any person constituted as we are, but whether any human being is actually looking at the object, or has looked at it, or will look at it, does not diminish the beauty of the object. Diderot's doctrine is that if a person who has both reason and sentiment were to look at it, then he would (given the ideal conditions which I shall examine in chapter 2) find it beautiful. But we shall now encounter a second contradiction, and one which is much more serious than the first.

Diderot distinguishes between *beau absolu* and *beau réel, beau aperçu* and *beau relatif*.[78] For the sake of clarity it might not be unwise to number these four sorts and spell out their differences.

1. *Beau absolu* denotes nothing but connotes something; that is to say, if there were no persons constituted as we are, that is with reason and sentiment, beauty would not exist. *Beau absolu* has no designation or denotation; beauty exists only if human beings exist. Diderot denies, therefore, the Platonic notion of objectively existing beauty.

2. *Beau réel* is used in two senses, though Diderot does not make this clear to the reader. *Beau réel* refers in the first

sense to objects that have the property of beauty, that is the capacity to awaken the notion of relationships in the understanding of anyone constituted as we are, provided that certain ideal conditions are met. Perrault's façade, then, would be a *beau réel* in the first sense. In the second sense, *beau réel* refers to a subset of *beau aperçu*. Therefore, I shall turn to that term before proceeding.

3. *Beau aperçu* is the actual state of the person in whom the object has excited and awakened various relations. These objects might be of two main classes: either one is considering an object by itself, such as a tulip, and one calls it beautiful without comparing it to other members of its genus or to the other genera of flowers; or one does compare it to others and calls it beautiful as an instance of the genus. The former class is, then, the *beau réel* in the second sense, i.e., objects considered on their own and relationships which hold within them; while the latter is *beau relatif*, i.e., objects considered in relation to members of the same family.

With these distinctions in hand, Diderot now asks the question, "Is it the reason or the sentiment that makes one aware of relations?"[79] His answer is a series of contradictions. The first is the following:

> When I say, "all that which awakens in me the idea of relationships," I do not mean that to call an object *beau* it is necessary to appreciate what sort of relationships reign in the object; I do not demand that he who sees a piece of architecture be in the position to say what even the architect might not have known—that this part has to this part a certain relation of a certain number to another number. . . . It suffices that he perceives and feels that the parts of this piece of architecture . . . have these relations either among themselves or with other objects.[80]

By means of the meager copula of *et* in "Il suffit qu'il aperçoive et sente," Diderot puts himself in a difficult position. He wants to hold that it is the understanding that perceives relationships, and this would be the natural conclusion to draw, given the radical dualism that he has posited between mind and body. He quickly tries to remedy the havoc caused by "It suffices that he perceive *and* feel," by mustering up a few tattered psychological soldiers—a practice very common among French philosophers of the eighteenth century when they found themselves in a philosophical discomfiture:

> It is the indetermination of these relationships, the facility
> of seizing them, and the pleasure which accompanies
> their perception, which have made us imagine that the
> *beau* was a matter of sentiment rather than of reason.
> . . . Whether a principle is known to us from our infancy,
> and which we have the habit of employing readily to
> objects outside of ourselves, we believe that we judge by
> sentiment, but we shall be constrained to admit our
> error whenever the contemplation of relationships and
> the novelty of the object suspend the application of the
> principle; in that case, pleasure will await to make itself
> felt until the understanding has pronounced that the
> object is *beau*.[81]

One is naturally led to ask why it was necessary to stipulate that *le beau* exists only for persons constituted as we are, that is, with reason and sentiment. If it is the reason that perceives the *rapports*, then would not sentiment be simply an embarrassment of riches? And if that is so, then it follows that *le beau absolu* would have not only a connotation but a denotation, supposing, of course, that there exist purely intellectual beings, or perhaps a species of being, on another planet that perform all the acrobatics of thought without suffering the confusions and discomforts of the feelings. But Diderot stoutly replies:

> Perception of relationships is, therefore, the foundation of the beautiful; it is, therefore, the perception of these relationships that one has designated in the various languages under an infinity of different terms, but which all indicate nothing other than different sorts of *beau*.[82]

It will be more fitting to examine the further consequences of Diderot's definition of *le beau* in the following chapter. But it is obvious that he cannot maintain at the same time that (1) *Le beau* exists only for persons constituted with mind and body; (2) It is reason and only reason that perceives the relationships which are the philosophical grounds of aesthetic beauty; and (3) It is not necessary that one understand or appreciate the relationships to feel the beauty of an object.

Although it is always pleasant and satisfying to give a summary of a matter dealt with at some length, I am afraid that it would be artificial and pointless to do so in the present case. We have observed a dozen variations on the same theme, and we have noticed their various complications and difficulties. What Descartes had bequeathed to the eighteenth century resembled other sorts of inheritances; one found oneself in possession of things which one did not really want, but which one felt obliged to keep either out of affection, a sense of loyalty, or of philosophical propriety.

II Rules and Spontaneity

Few periods in Western civilization have accorded as much interest and importance to the fine arts as the French Enlightenment. Given the rise of analytic thought in France during the seventeenth century, it was only natural that persons of a philosophical bent should begin to reflect seriously about the creation and appreciation of the fine arts. The second great theme that haunted the French aestheticians of the eighteenth century was the nature and function of rules. One might explain on three grounds why this theme was of such importance during the period.

First, many of the aestheticians of the period were competent mathematicians and physicists, at least according to the standards of the day. André and Batteux, for example, wrote texts on physiology, mathematics, and certain parts of physics. Many of the same writers were also determinists; they held that all events, both in the natural world and in the spiritual, proceeded in accordance with invariable laws. Of course the pious genuflection was usually made to man's personal freedom, and his subsequent guilt for having broken one of God's laws, but when the writers whom we are studying pursued a subject seriously, they did so as determinists or mechanists. Given the great rise of physics in the seventeenth century, it was natural to assume that man's aesthetic experience must be governed, in some way or another, by laws. Furthermore, even the productions of genius must in some way fall under the immutable laws either of climate and heredity or of psychology. But, as we shall see, the role of rules according to many writers was equivocal, tenuous, and vague.

Secondly, the writers whom we are discussing were members of one of the most formalistic societies that have ever existed. Some of them belonged to the middling ranks of the aristocracy, and many others were men of the cloth. When one considers the elaborate rituals of the court, of the church, of gatherings in salons, of the etiquette of letters and dedications to books, of the forms of addressing and taking leave of someone encountered in a public building, of courting and making love; when one thinks of all those exquisite forms that came to their maturity during the first two-thirds of the eighteenth century, it is only reasonable to assume that persons who lived during the period should assume that the fine arts must also be closely allied to rules, laws, and unbreachable forms. This is, of course, only a genetic argument for explaining the importance of rules to the eighteenth-century aesthetician, but that is exactly what I intend it to be.

Thirdly, because of the explorations and writings of Winckelmann and other persons interested in the Greek and Roman antiquities, the educated man in the eighteenth century caught sight, so to speak, of a new planet. It was as if another world had existed very close to our own but had never before been perceived. The world of the ancient Greeks and Romans was very different from the one known to the eighteenth century. The arts of antiquity seemed to be governed by strict laws of symmetry, purity of line, balance, and clarity. It was not that the eighteenth century was unacquainted with other civilizations or other epochs. China and Japan had long been discovered, and the Chinese taste, for better or worse, had crept in here and there in French furniture and decoration. The arts of the New World had also been discovered, but they were more like curios and oddities that one keeps in an *armoire bibliothèque* or a curio cabinet.

The eighteenth century was only too well acquainted with certain periods of its predecessors. The loathing that the Enlightenment felt toward the Gothic is well known. Crousaz, for example, says that as soon as the principles of order and symmetry became known, the *colifichets* or the gewgaws of the Gothic style fell into disrepute. Even though the eighteenth century might have idealized the Greek and Roman worlds, and even though they doubtless often misunderstood and misinterpreted the findings of antiquity, the cultivated man of the French Enlightenment found himself face to face with a finished civilization—both in the sense that it no longer existed and also in the sense that it was believed to be perfect. It was only another step to elevate the ancient world of the Greeks and Romans into an ideal and to try to infer certain rules of universal purport.

Though there are doubtless other reasons or causes of the interest in rules, these seem to be the most germane. What might have given the final impetus to the many discussions on the subject was the irritating recurrence of the *je ne sais quoi* whenever one tried to explain why one appreciated a certain work of art or to explain why a certain artist had failed or succeeded. The *je ne sais quoi* made its appearance whenever an author found himself embarrassed about liking something without being able to give a reason. Although this sort of embarrassment rarely occurs among persons of our own period, who seem to pride themselves on their speechlessness, it was a distinct source of pain for the Age of Reason. One finds the *je ne sais quoi* over and over again in Bouhours; one finds it even in such exacting writers as Montesquieu:

> There is sometimes in persons and in things an invisible
> charm, a sort of natural grace which one cannot define
> and which one is forced to call the *je ne sais quoi*. It

seems to me that it is an effect principally founded on surprise. We are moved that a person can please us more than we had at first thought that he ought to please us, and we are agreeably surprised that he has been able to conquer the defects that we first distinguished.[1]

The *je ne sais quoi* seemed to be a concession to the irrational and the indefinable.[2] In effect it was a denial of the supremacy of reason over the sentiments and feelings. Even more seriously, the *je ne sais quoi* opened the doors to vagueness, liberalism, and social change. It was, therefore, an element to be combated for philosophical and political reasons.

The first few attempts to combat it were hazy and little more than echoes of Plato, Aristotle, and St. Augustine. Crousaz tells us that the three principles—regularity, order, and proportion—are necessary and sufficient criteria for aesthetic value. He has, it is true, another theory, which is utilitarian in tone, but I shall defer discussion of it until later on in the chapter when I shall deal at length with Crousaz's notions about rules. Let us note in passing that Crousaz holds that

variety, therefore, essentially pleases the human mind; it is a principle of experience. The mind is made for variety, and variety animates it, keeps it from falling into ennui, and into languor. But one also has to have unity amid variety, without which this diversity would fatigue and confuse the mind; one needs both the one and the other.[3]

André for the most part simply echoes St. Augustine: *Omnis porro pulchritudinis forma unitas est.*[4] A. de Marcenay de Ghuy, in his slender *Essai sur la beauté* (1770), says, "Beauty is founded on the correctness of proportions, of which the harmonious cooperation forms an entirety as perfect as possible."[5] Briseux, in the *Traité du beau essentiel dans les arts* (1752), which is chiefly devoted to architecture, says simply, "One will give birth to true beauties only if one subjects oneself to the eternal laws of wise nature in its proportions."[6]   However, instead of giving a simple inventory of the thought concerning laws and spontaneity, it will be best to clarify how aestheticians of the period conceived of aesthetic laws and to show the various assumptions and modes of argument that they commonly employed.

After a survey of the writings on the fine arts, one can safely conclude that the French aestheticians of the eighteenth century tended to conceive of aesthetic rules or laws under seven distinct heads.   At the risk of pedantry, I shall number them:

1.   An aesthetic rule is a general proposition, having a subject and a predicate; the copula, however, is not a form of the verb "to be," or its equivalent in any other language.   The rule asserts something about an entire set of objects.   For example, "All tragedies should represent actions which take place during a day and a night and only that."   Or, to infer an example from a passage in Fontenelle, "Eclogues should be written in language and should employ ideas that one would naturally expect from pastoral people; the dialogue should not be courtly, and the subject matter should be neither philosophical nor religious."

2.   An aesthetic rule is imperative in tone, and the copula, therefore, is related to "should be" or "ought to be" or "must be."   A rule is a direction or an indication for some kind of human behavior.   It has the tone of advice given to someone who is not doing what he should be doing or not doing it well enough.

3.   Given the second trait of aesthetic rule, it is only natural, especially in the light of the long debate between reason and sentiment which we have already suffered through, to conclude that an aesthetic rule must be related to human nature.   The rules are directed to persons who have reason,

lumière, feelings, and body. It would be idle to erect aesthetic rules for persons who are not constituted as we are or to demand of defective persons that they obey them. If one is said to be obliged to follow a certain aesthetic rule, one must be capable of doing so.

4. An aesthetic rule is a proposition to which one is personally committed, that is, a rule which one is willing to argue for, to act in accordance with, and to hold stoutly. Although eighteenth-century aestheticians in France did not employ the word *autonome*, they frequently contrasted the person who simply follows a rule because it is the thing to do or in vogue with the person who believes for his own part that the rule is worthy of his following it. Doubtless, as many writers were to remark, one might teach children the rules of *bon goût*. Children might at first simply imitate their teacher's example. Furthermore, someone might have such bad taste that he must always rely upon other persons' verdicts and other persons' rules. Ideally, however, an aesthetic rule is autonomous. Whether its foundation is objective or relative—and I shall turn to this distinction in a few moments—writers of the period held that the rules of good taste should be rules that one holds because of their intrinsic reasonableness. Although one might marshal the testimony of Aristotle or St. Augustine by way of support or example, the force of the rule lies within its own power over one's reason.

5. Aesthetic rules, unlike the laws of physics, can be obeyed or disobeyed. One is simply governed by the laws of one's machine and by the laws of the universe. But aesthetic laws can be breached, either willfully—(by an act of flagrant bad taste or by the rights of genius), or nonvoluntarily (by negligence or simple ignorance). An aesthetic rule is, therefore, something that can dictate a course of action that is contrary to the natural bent of human nature. Aesthetic rules can ameliorate, refine, and deepen aesthetic sensibility.

6. All writers of the period agreed that an aesthetic rule

or principle should be helpful, either to the artist who is making a work of art or to the critic or amateur who is interested in appreciating it. As we shall see, certain writers held that aesthetic rules are, as a matter of fact, not helpful to either critics or artists. But as I have already mentioned, I am now describing what philosophers of the period understood by aesthetic rule. Whether there actually exist such rules, or whether a certain philosopher believed that they did not exist, is a separate question and will be dealt with later on in this chapter.

7. The last trait of an aesthetic rule is difficult to describe, but it might be put in the following way. Let us suppose that there was a set of rules which fit all the six requirements already mentioned, and let us suppose that we describe them in full to a certain person who is very much like Watteau's "L'Indifférent." He might say: "Yes, how interesting. But what does all that have to do with me?" An aesthetic rule must be the sort of rule which, once it is well understood, becomes a principle for someone; he is spurred on by it, he wants to act in accordance with it. The seventh trait is not the same as the third trait, i.e., that aesthetic rules are related to human nature or to one's feelings. One might know that a certain principle did have certain effects upon one's feelings or aesthetic sensibility but not be moved to act or to put oneself in the position to appreciate the work. It is paradoxical to speak of someone having a principle in accordance with which he never acts. One would say of such a person that he can parrot the principles that other persons hold or that he is a hypocrite. An aesthetic principle, then, is a rule that spurs one on or tends to do so. If it is a valid rule, it should not leave one indifferent.

I do not mean to imply that any particular aesthetician of the Enlightenment spelled out these seven traits in such detail; however, the general tone and bent of the arguments surrounding the numerous disputes concerning the nature of rules lead me to conclude that these are the defining traits of aesthetic rule for the writers of the period. Secondly, though all the writers of the period tended to mean the same thing by "rule," they fell into three main camps. Before dealing with particular philosophers, I should like to describe each of these camps in turn.

There was a small group who held that the only kinds of rules are for what one might call in twentieth-century philosophical language "rules for closed classes," that is, a set of rules which are both necessary and sufficient for asserting that a certain object has or does not have a certain aesthetic value, and secondly, that the members of this class are finite and nonexpandable. For examples of rules for closed classes, one might turn to the entire collection of Greek pottery, including all those discovered, and those to be discovered; or again the entire class of Roman frescoes, including all those in museums and those still under whitewash. Consequently, if a critic wanted to appraise a member of a given closed class, he would have to know the necessary and sufficient criteria, or if someone wanted to imitate a certain style exactly, the artist-imitator would have to know the standards. I should like to call persons who held that such rules exist *antiquarians*. This does not do any violence to the word. If an art were still living, one would not want to set limits to it, for one would not be sure what new direction it might take. But the antiquarian, even though he might be presented with a new specimen which will lead him to alter certain of his requirements, is always retrospective. A good example of the antiquarian among the writers with whom we are dealing is Madame Dacier, a lady of unusual erudition and consummate ignorance. As we shall see, if Madame Dacier had had her way, all art would have been imitative of Homer and certain other Greek writers. Madame Dacier was the aggressive antiquarian; there were others, more meek and genteel, who did not try to convert their contemporaries to the rules that they had inferred, rightly or wrongly, from antiquity.

But most aestheticians of the period were either *absolutists* or *relativists* in regard to rules. They assumed, to use once again the language of logic, that such rules refer to "open" classes—classes whose members cannot be enumerated because they are potentially infinite in number. The antiquarian thought that the artist could at best only imitate the "closed" world of the Greek or Roman artist. But the absolutist and the relativist held that rules applied in general to all men, although men widely differed on the ways they applied.

The writers—and we shall examine them in detail in a few moments—who believed that aesthetic rules are absolute or objective generally held the following tenets:

1. An aesthetic rule is discovered by reason or at least by a special kind of "sensible reason." If the senses are required to know the rules, it is simply because the mind often needs visible or audible examples in order to learn. Just as a diagram helps someone learning geometry, so the beauties of nature or a beautiful work of art help someone learning aesthetic rules. Or, to put the same point in a slightly different way, when one asserts an aesthetic rule, all of one's reasons are to be introduced by such verb forms as "knowing," "apprehending," or "understanding clearly that." One would not employ such expressions as "I feel that" or "Sentiment leads me to believe."

2. Aesthetic rules are inalterable. Even though societies change and entire civilizations crumble, human reason remains steadfast. Therefore, given the first tenet it must be that aesthetic rules are on the same plane as those of geometry rather than those of the customs and institutions of particular peoples.

3. From the two preceding tenets one would naturally be led to assert that aesthetic rules are universal or the same for all cultures. Although the eighteenth-century aesthetician was well acquainted with the variety of cultures—the taste for the exotic was extreme during the first two-thirds of the period—nevertheless, the objectivists held that there exist certain principles which are, as a matter of fact, the same for all cultures.

55

4. Given these dicta, it is only a short step to assuming that the rules of taste are applicable to particular works of art in a purely syllogistic or deductive manner. The major premise would state an aesthetic principle; the minor premise would describe the particular work of art or object in nature, and the conclusion would tell us whether the object was aesthetically good or bad or neither.

5. The last tenet of the absolutist could readily be anticipated by anyone who had followed the bent of the previous four. Although aesthetic rules might admit of refinements and stipulations, they do not admit of exceptions. One encounters in certain of the writers whom we are studying a sort of aesthetic casuistry. We find the same straining to save the general principles of *le bon goût* and to do justice to particular works of art that one finds in certain writers who figured in the Counter Reformation, such as Suarez. It is true that a rule does not become less universal by becoming more precise. One might state the conditions of when the people have not only the right but the obligation to rise up and kill their leaders—a period of long suppression, foreign and threatening states allied with the rulers against the people, the infeasability of parliamentary change, etc.—even though these conditions may rarely be met. It is not, therefore, the paucity of factual events that renders a rule nonuniversal. We shall see, however, that this fifth tenet was to cause considerable confusion and discomfiture among the absolutists. Let us leave them now and turn to the third camp.

What the relativists lack in rigor they often make up for in charm. It would not be unjust to describe the aesthetic relativist of the period as one who maintained three chief principles. When I say "maintained" I do not mean to imply that any particular writer explicitly enunciated these three principles in the form of a manifesto. Nothing can be further removed from the aesthetic temperament in France during the Regency and under Louis XV than straightforwardness, directness of statement, or unveiled assertion. When I say that the relativists *maintained* certain principles, I mean that after a good reading of their works, one is fairly certain that the following were their assumptions.

First, the relativist, as one would naturally expect, was greatly struck by the diversity of tastes, not only from one civilization to another but from one period of the same civilization to the next and even from a man's youth to his middle age. The first principle is, then, simply a factual one; there is a great variety and diversity of tastes.

The second principle, however, is not factual. The relativist of the period wanted to hold that there is no way or method of deciding who is in the right. One can indulge in mutual recrimination, in calumny—the French Enlightenment is studded with some of the most vicious satire ever written—but one cannot prove that one's own verdict is right, and one cannot logically prove that one's opponent is wrong.

The third and last principle is fairly innocent; let each man have his own taste—a plea for aesthetic egalitarianism. If a man stoutly believes that a certain painter is of value, and if he clutters his walls with the artist's works, even though we might not care to visit the man in the intimacy of his salon, we should not mock him or lampoon him in front of his enemies.

It might not be out of place to make a few general remarks concerning the position of the eighteenth-century aesthetic relativist. It is evident that the third principle is compatible with the position of the objectivist. A man of the latter camp might also be inclined not to argue with a man who did not share his aesthetic views, simply because it is often boorish to argue or because of that permeating lassitude that one sometimes feels when one is struck by the pointlessness of discussion. The absolutist might even go so far as to encourage the man whose taste he finds vicious and corrupt, just as one sometimes encourages persons with their eccentricities so that they do not fall into an even greater evil. Consequently, since the third principle is compatible with both absolutism and relativism, it is not a defining characteristic of the latter, even though one encounters aesthetic liberalism more frequently among the relativists than among the absolutists. Aesthetic tolerance might exist in either camp.

As for the first principle—that taste varies—one might say that it is interesting but does not prove the relativity of aesthetic rules. Many aestheticians of the eighteenth century, however, maintained that if the first principle is true, then the second must be so also. Saint-Evremond, for example, argued that[7]

> one presents us with an infinity of rules made three thousand years ago to regulate what is going on today; one does not realize that it is not the same subject that one must deal with today nor the same kind of spirit that leads us. If we made love in the same way as Anacreon and Sappho, nothing could be more ridiculous, in the same way as Terence, nothing more bourgeois, like Lucien, nothing more gross. All times have their own character which is peculiar to them, their interests, and their business; they have their morality in some manner having their faults and their virtues. It is always man, but human nature varies, and art is nothing more than an imitation of nature and, therefore, must vary as does nature. Our stupidities are not the same ones that Horace ridiculed; our vices are not the same ones that Juvenal condemned. We must employ a different kind of ridicule and a different kind of censure.[8]

Many writers thought that climate greatly influenced the fine arts, and since climate varies so must taste. We shall examine the various arguments advanced for the first principle in detail, but it is obvious that even if it were true, principle two, which is normative in tone, would not necessarily follow. One might readily admit that taste varies but not be compelled to grant that there is no way of adjudicating matters of taste. We might imagine a planet composed of troglodytes, and in each cave a hermit is working on his own mathematics; unfortunately, the systems are jointly incompatible. One would not, therefore, infer that mathematical truth does not exist. Consequently, though the first principle might have some anthropological or sociological interest, it has no philosophical importance.

It follows, then, that the heart of the eighteenth-century version of aesthetic relativism must lie in the second principle, that is, there is no way of deciding about matters of taste. But this principle admits also of a number of modifications and species. It might be best to give a brief catalog of them before proceeding to the writers in question.

Firstly, certain writers tried to show that the second principle is true by producing examples of persons who agree about the attributes and traits of a certain work of art, but who disagree about its worth. Clearly, to have a genuine disagreement or agreement the two persons must be talking about the same work, and they must have the same beliefs about its physical attributes. I shall call this the *argument by perfect example*.

Secondly, other writers tried to prove the second principle by arguing that one learns what is in good taste and what is not simply by imitation of one's betters. Since infancy and early youth are the most intense periods of imitation, and since everyone was at some time young, the aesthetic taste of mankind is a long series of imitations. I shall call this the *argument by learning*.

Finally, one encounters an argument, that I should like to call *argumentum ad lassitudinem*. For my own part, I find it extremely persuasive. One becomes so weary of attempts to show that a certain thing is really something else and so accustomed to seeing why each proposal falters or fails, that one has to refute the author by a yawn. Certain aestheticians of the eighteenth century realized that mankind was no longer young, and that there had been a plethora of aesthetic rules proposed. None worked. They were either so broad as to encompass everything or so specific that they described only a particular work of art. The natural result is a general lassitude, a tepid scepticism concerning any so-called "aesthetic rule."

I should like to turn now to particular writers of the Enlightenment both to illustrate the distinctions that I have noted above and to follow the intricacies of their arguments. Since Batteux was in many respects the aesthetic spokesman of the period, one might do well to begin with him.

In the *avant-propos* to his *Les Beaux-Arts réduits à un même principe,* he asserts that everyone is always complaining about the multitude of rules, and that rules annoy both the author who wants to write and the amateur who wants to judge. Nonetheless, Batteux wants to hold that laws both exist and are useful. "The rules have been multiplied by observations made upon works, and the rules should be simplified by bringing these observations back to a common principle."[9]

Batteux suggests that one imitate physicists who amass many experiments in order to establish a sole hypothesis or theory.

> This principle would establish in one blow the true genius
> and would free it from a thousand vain scruples in order
> to subject it to one and only one sovereign law, which,
> once well understood, would be the basis, the outline,
> and the justification of all the rules.[10]

Although such an undertaking might seem a little bold, Batteux hopes to find a sole principle which will act as the chief guide for the artist and the final court of appeal for the critic. Anyone who is even passingly acquainted with the history of philosophy might have a number of reservations about such an enterprise. Attempts to show *the* nature of truth, or *the* nature of ethical goodness, or *the* nature of knowledge have always failed, even though the particular failures have often been greatly illuminating. And so one might be tempted to invoke the *argumentum ad lassitudinem* against Batteux and set his rather cumbersome book aside. But let us hear him out and see what the *même principe is*.

It would not be out of place at this time to ask why Batteux believes that there must be—for he says *doivent se simplifier*—a sole principle. There are a number of reasons for this belief. First, as I have already mentioned, Batteux was passionately interested in mathematics and in physics, much more so—judging from the examples he presents in *Les Beaux-Arts réduits* —than in aesthetics and the fine arts. Since one tried to start from a first principle in the physics of Batteux's day, it was only natural, given his scientific training, to attempt the same method in aesthetics. Secondly, even though one should be wary of invoking "the spirit of the age" and similar terms, one might remember that France had become a highly centralized and bureaucratic society by the time Batteux was writing. He was born in 1713 and died in 1780. The sole principle of French society, the Sun King, died two years after Batteux was born, and during the Regency the court withdrew from Versailles. Paris became not only the seat of the court but the seat of government. Paris became and remained not only the chief city of France but the sole city. But thirdly, to give a more philosophical explanation of his certainty that the fine arts can be reduced to a sole principle, Batteux tries to show that the fine arts are autonomous, that is, that they have a foundation, and a function, which is peculiar to them. He wants to prove that the fine arts cannot be reduced to some other human endeavor, such as science or religion. Certain aestheticians who were contemporaries of Batteux attempted to convince the reader that the fine arts are really a form of moral instruction, or really a form of understanding the processes of nature, or really a means to simple sensuous pleasure. Batteux assumes that if the fine arts are autonomous, then there must be one and only one principle which serves as their foundation. If there were more than one principle, he seems to assume that the fine arts would be heteronomous, i.e., that their *raison d'être* would be to inform *and* to give pleasure *and* to give moral instruction. If there were many principles, then the fine arts, so Batteux appears to believe, would have many points in common with other human activities. If that were so, he concludes that the fine arts would not have an *essence* or something which is peculiar to them. Finally, if this last proposition were true, Batteux would conclude that one cannot give a justification of the fine arts. Therefore, since he is bent on giving an apologia, he must find a sole principle.

Since it is all too easy to spot the fallaciousness of Batteux's assumptions, I shall let the matter rest with a brief commentary. There are many human activities and endeavors which do not have an essence or sole principle peculiar to them but which, nonetheless, are of consummate importance. A number of traits might serve to characterize and delimit a certain activity, though none of these traits is peculiar to every aspect of the activity, and each trait might be shared with some other endeavor. Polyphyletic definitions, if I may be permitted the term, are generally of far greater help in defining such terms as "art," "moral goodness," and "reality" than essentialist definitions. But let us return to Batteux.

Because his principle is intimately related to his theory of imitation, part of the discussion of his principle will be treated in the next chapter on imitation and creation. Roughly put, Batteux held that all true art and only true art consists in the imitation of *la belle nature*. I shall translate that term as "ideal nature" for various reasons which will soon be made clear. The imitation of nature is the end of all the arts, and they differ among themselves only in their various means of imitating. The rules of taste are nothing but the consequences of the principles of imitation. He argues that if the arts are essentially imitations of *la belle nature,* it follows that taste consists in knowing the ideals of nature. Man, so Batteux reasons, choses among nature's products; he does not imitate nature as it actually exists. Aesthetic values, then, rest upon the artist's having well chosen and imitated well. Speaking of artistic genius he says, "They are creatures designed for observing, and, reciprocally, they are observers only to be capable of creating; . . . genius has no limits in regard to objects, other than those of the universe."[11] If one should ask why the artist should imitate nature, Batteux would reply that only nature contains the plans for regular, symmetrical, and harmonious work. Art does not create its rules but derives them from *la belle nature.*[12]

Now this principle is hardly new, and Batteux, who was a man of the world, knew so as well. He admits that Plato and Aristotle invoked a similar principle, but he hoped to refine upon it. *La belle nature* is "not that which exists, but that which could exist; it is the ideal truth represented as if it actually existed and with all the perfections of which it is susceptible."[13] It is now

> easy to define the arts of which we have spoken up to
> this point. One knows their object, their purpose, their
> function, and the manner in which they are dealt with;
> what they have in common, and what each has peculiar
> to it. . . . One defines painting, sculpture, or dance as
> an imitation of *la belle nature* expressed by colors, by
> relief, by gestures. And music and poetry are the imita-
> tion of ideal nature expressed by sounds and by measured
> discourse.[14]

Batteux stipulates that to judge whether ideal nature has been well imitated or not depends on the interest of the object to human ends and desires. One might be inclined to call this assertion tautological, but I think it is not. Batteux appears to hold that certain members of the class "ideal nature" are interesting because they have a distinct rapport with human lives and institutions. It is such things as these that the artist should imitate. His theory becomes more elaborate:

> Taste is an acquaintance with the rules by means of sentiment. This way of knowing them is much more fine and much more sure than the way in which the mind knows, and even without the knowledge [*connaissance*] of the rules all the lights of the mind are almost useless to someone who wants to compose.[15]

He continues in the same vein in chapter 6, entitled "That There Are Particular Rules for Each Work," and proceeds to tell us that aesthetic rules are inadequate: "Who will tell me when I should begin an image and when I should finish it, and where I should place it? The examples set by the great Masters?"[16] If that were so, as Batteux rightly holds, one would produce only imitations. It is taste "which will guide genius in the invention of details,"[17] and taste is itself guided by nature, "And if you are not capable of reading nature yourself, I could say to you, 'Withdraw, the domain is sacred'."[18]

Batteux says that if worst comes to worst, read the masters, the ancients, and imitate them. If you have no talent yourself, at least you will not fall into bad taste by carefully imitating the masters. But "remember that a small number of persons suffices to create the models for the rest of the human race."[19]

After reading the preceding quotations, I believe two complaints naturally come to mind: (1) Why should aesthetic feelings be so sure and certain? Why should aesthetic feelings be infallible? and (2) How can there be particular rules for each work of art? I should like to deal with these two questions separately before proceeding with Batteux's theory.

1. Although we have already discussed many of the problems surrounding the dualism of reason and sentiment, we

might ask what it would mean to speak of knowing a rule by sentiment rather than by one's mind. At some points Batteux implies that it is a question of degree. The mind can never reach an intensity of belief without the stimulus of the sentiments. At other points he seems to imply that there are two distinct ways of knowing an aesthetic rule, i.e., either by reason or by sentiment. It is obvious, of course, that "knowing by means of the reason" differs in one way from "knowing by means of the sentiments." Though it might be true or false that someone does know something by means of the sentiment, that which he knows "by the reason" may be true or false, but that which he feels "by the sentiments" could be neither true nor false. Beliefs might be true or false, sentiments are neither the one nor the other, except in the sense in which we speak of "genuine" sentiments as opposed to those which are "trumped up" or "artificial."

Though sentiments are neither true nor false referentially, they might be falsely, though sincerely, held. For example, let us imagine a man who has all the furies of love, all the symptoms, and ardently believes that he is in love with a certain woman. Nothing offends a lover more than to doubt that he is in love. But how can he be so sure? By introspection? That would reveal only a chaos of sentiments and memories. Still, he is sure that he is in love. What is needed is an experiment contrived, perhaps, by the woman whom he sincerely believes he loves. It should be an experiment that involves a great risk on his part, or a great undertaking, or perhaps something quite simple, a certain gesture, or recollection, or regard. Then suddenly he sees that he is no longer in love. Vanity will lead him to believe that he truly was, but that things have changed. To avoid further rhapsody on this point, let us observe that there is nothing about sentiments that makes them infallible. Though they are not true or false by reference, they can be falsely or truly held. Therefore, if there are such things as aesthetic sentiments, as Batteux holds, there is no ground for saying that they are more sure than knowledge or belief. Notice how much language is shared by reason and sentiment; both reason and sentiment can "deceive" one, both reason and sentiment can "compel" one to do so-and-so, and one can strongly hold a certain proposition either on grounds of reason —as in physics—or on the grounds of sentiment—as in love or friendship.

2. When Batteux writes of aesthetic rules which are peculiar to each work of art, one is forced to admit that he is either contradicting himself or indulging in paradox. As we have seen, the notion of "generality" is included in the notion of "aesthetic rule." It may be true that there are no aesthetic rules at all, but this is not Batteux's position. He holds that rules exist, and that certain of them, if not the majority, apply to particular works of art and are not generalizable. It is a rule for Louis XV *boiseries* that if the top of the door edging is curved, then the two top panels of the door must also have curved lines which preserve the same degree of curve as the top edging, and, secondly, the bottom two panels of the door should be only half the length of the two top panels. This is an example of an aesthetic rule, though, of course, not one of Batteux's; furthermore, the rule is not vitiated by the existence of few pure Louis XV *boiseries*. However, a rule which applies and can only apply to one work of art involves a misuse of the word "rule." But the charge of self-contradiction is all too easy to make and not too gallant. I suppose the following is what Batteux has in mind when he speaks of rules that can have only one referent. When we appreciate a work of art, we appreciate *it*, and not some properties that it may or may not have in common with others. Our fondness of works of art is akin to our fondness of persons; it is their intense particularity that attracts us. There are thousands of paintings of the Deposition of Christ, of Venus, and of the Assumption of the Virgin, but that fact does not lessen our interest in and esteem for Rembrandt's *Deposition*, or Botticelli's *Venus*, or

Murillo's *Assumption*. Although one can give reasons for liking a work of art, there comes a time when one can say no more. Still, it is true that Batteux would have caused less confusion had he not used the word "rule" when writing about the uniqueness of works of art.

Batteux explains the varieties of taste by invoking the richness of nature on the one side and the limitations of the human mind and heart on the other. Since there is only one *belle nature*, there can be only one true taste, but *la belle nature* is so immense and abundant that artists will never weary of imitating her. Batteux uses an image which is now well worn, but which had luster in his day. Nature is like a model in an artist's studio, around which a dozen young draftsmen are making sketches from different points of view. The various drawings would not contradict one another but rather complement each other. Batteux concludes with a flourish of liberalism, "And so let it be that everyone has his own taste, provided that it is modeled on some part of nature."[20]

During the course of his book the *même principe* actually becomes two principles or perhaps three:

> In effect, both in nature and in the arts things touch us in proportion as they have some relation to us; it follows that works which have the double rapport of agreeableness and of utility will be more touching than those which have only one of the two.[21]

The final statement of his theory would be that the fine arts must: (1) imitate *la belle nature*, (2) do so agreeably, and (3) have some utility for human beings. But let us turn away from Batteux, who tends to be of the absolutists' camp, to Saint-Evremond, who tends to be of the relativists'.

In a letter to the Duchess of Mazarin,[22] Saint-Evremond strikes a pose which was rare for the period. Though he admired the ancient Greek and Roman writers, he refused to be subjected by them. Aesthetic rules, whatever they might be, have not been and never would be like the laws of physics:

> I want the spirit of the ancients to inspire us, but I do
> not want us to adopt the same spirit. I want them to
> teach us how to think well, but I do not like to make
> use of their ideas. What we find among them had the
> grace of novelty when it was made; what we write today
> has aged from century to century and has fallen as
> if extinct in the understanding of our authors.[23]

He is only a step away from aesthetic relativism, and he takes that step in the following passage: "The change of religion, of government, of mores, of manners, has made such a great change in the world that we must have, so to speak, a new art in order to enter into the taste and spirit of the century in which we live."[24]

We might divide the aesthetic relativists of the period into three camps: (1) the *futilists*, or those who held the position of relativism and at the same time held that the fine arts decay and lose their interest as science progresses; (2) the *optimists*, or those who held that the fine arts progress in some sense comparable to the developments of physics and mathematics; and (3) the *cyclicists*, or those who held that the rise, flourishing, and fall of the fine arts parallel the rise and fall of civilizations, and that the history of the world is like the history of waves breaking on a beach. Saint-Evremond was evidently a futilist, for he asserts: "The spirit of the age is opposed to the spirit of fables and false mysteries. We like the open truth, and good sense prevails over the illusions of fantasy; only solidity and reason content us today."[25]

The age of poetry is dead, Saint-Evremond argues, because the sciences are finally alive and growing. It is only primitive people who take delight in far-fetched comparisons and mysterious happenings. Saint-Evremond particularly criticized the poets who were trying to imitate the ancients:

> Our poets have not had the strength to leave the gods, nor the capability to make use of what our own religion might furnish them with. Attached to the taste of the ancients and necessitated by our sentiments, they have given the appearance of Mercury to our angels and that of fabulous mysteries to our miracles.[26]

If poetry and imaginative literature in general are to have a continuing interest in an age of science they must, Saint-Evremond holds, radically change their subjects. Fictions must be banished; good sense must be introduced.

One has considerable sympathy with Saint-Evremond's position, for the bulk of eighteenth-century French poetry is a deadly bore. One reads it in school but rereads it only under duress. The poetry that one returns to has a sharpness and truthfulness akin to science. Although one might not want to follow Saint-Evremond as far as his final conclusion—that imaginative literature will ultimately disappear once science has a firm hold over mankind—one would grant that we demand a new tone from poetry and a greater relevance.

As for rules in general, Saint-Evremond holds that all admit of exceptions. "One must admit that the *Poetics* of Aristotle is an excellent work; however, there is nothing so perfect that it can serve as a rule for all times and in all nations."[27] He argues that it is only men of little talent who strictly follow the rules; genius not only does but must make exceptions to them. Irregularity is not only the right but the hallmark of genius. Aesthetic spontaneity, according to Saint-Evremond, is not the discovery of new aesthetic rules but the actual creation of new objects.

Other writers of the period were stout absolutists. C. E. Briseux, in his *Traité du beau essentiel dans les arts*, asserts:

> Can genius suffer to be shackled and imprisoned by rules? Would it not suffocate its fire to fix limits to the sphere of its activity? No, the arts are not imprisoned

by being given rules; it is the form of its productions. Without this precaution, of what extravagances is it not capable, and to what excesses of caprice might it not allow itself to be carried away?[28]

Briseux explains the differences of taste in two ways:

The first is born from the degree of the capability and sentiment of the observer. . . . The second depends upon the state of the organs which might be well or ill disposed, the impression of the object being always in accordance with the organ that receives it, and often the images of objects are disfigured by the defectiveness of the sense upon which the images leave their impression.[29]

Briseux soon leaves philosophy for architecture, which was his true interest. It is not surprising, therefore, that the sections on architecture in this book, and particularly the plates of the villas of Count Valerio Chiericato and Count Valmanara at Venice are of greater interest than his philosophy.

Of all the great ladies of the eighteenth century, of all the *femmes savantes*, none was more formidable, more aggressive, or more dull than Madame Dacier. She was, of course, an absolutist:

But during the last fifty years there has arisen, I do not want to say a set of pygmies, but of men who are very mediocre, who without any other weapons than their boldness (for not one of them knows Greek), have raised their standard against this great poet.[30]

Madame Dacier is speaking of Homer, and the particular "pygmy" in question was de la Motte, who had dared to criticize him. He had written that one finds numerous fictions in Homer, which are piled one upon the other and interspersed with boring episodes, gods suddenly appearing to save not only the characters from disaster but the poet from acute embarrassment, long and tedious narrations; in short, de la Motte had simply said a few things that are true about *The Iliad* and *The Odyssey*. But Madame Dacier does not share this belief: "We have seen in a convincing manner that it is the study of the Greek and Latin authors which has pulled us out of the grossness in which we lay."[31]

Madame Dacier asserts that "we have seen," but she ought to have said, "I command you to believe," for her evidence is as shaky as it is ludicrous. Although she believes that there are other causes of the bad taste that had recently swept over France—bad education, licentious spectacles, frivolous writings, and the insouciance of youth—it is chiefly ignorance of the Greek and Latin masters, so Madame Dacier holds, that has done the century in.

A. Houdard de la Motte was both a mild and perspicacious man, but, since his opponent had neither of these virtues, it would be tedious to follow the endless chain of her accusations and his responses. It is easier to see de la Motte's position in regard to aesthetic rules by citing his response to Voltaire,[32] who was, in regard to the "unities," an absolutist:

> I shall say further, sir, that the unity of interest is independent of the three other unities, since in the *Cid*, there is neither unity of time, place, nor action, and, nonetheless, unity of interest is there. . . . The interest, for example, of *Bérénice* is too small. Will Titus marry her? Will he not marry her? The event is one of the most familiar, and it is upon this fault that a certain pleasantry was common during Racine's day:
> > "Marion pleure, Marion crie,
> > Marion veut qu'on la marie."[33]

La Motte sees that the only true aesthetic principle is interest; Aristotle's so-called "unities" are subsidiary to the principle of interest. According to la Motte, the only aesthetic crime is boredom; anything is excusable as long as one's interest does not flag.

Fontenelle, who writes with a delicacy and finesse that reminds one of Watteau, shares la Motte's sentiment that rules are of little use to the artist and are often a hindrance to the critic. In his "Discours sur la nature de l'eclogue," Fontenelle says:

> The eclogues preceded the reflections; I wrote, and then I thought—and though it is to the shame of reason, this is what generally happens. And so I should not be surprised if one finds that I have not followed my own rules, for I did not know them well when I wrote; moreover, it is much easier to make rules than to follow them, and it seems to be established by usage that one does not necessitate the other.[34]

Madame Dacier's imperious absolutism in regard to aesthetic rules had become as cold and funereal as the court of Versailles during the last years of Louis XIV. Some persons mocked the rules, like Monsieur le Prince, who, after being told that the Abbé d'Aubignac had written the only tragedy that conformed to the rules of Aristotle, asserted that he was grateful to Monsignor Aubignac for following Aristotle's rules, but he could not pardon Aristotle's rules for having made Monsignor Aubignac write a wretched tragedy. Other persons tried to save appearances by arguing that the rules must exist, but that they are unknown or very difficult to know. Taillasson, for example, in his philosophical poem "Le Danger des règles dans les arts," asserts in the preface:

> There are in the fine arts rules to which one ought to subject oneself, but it is quite difficult to determine them, and the great talents have proved how arbitrary the rules are. If there is a small number of good rules that

nature indicates, there is a crowd of rules which are useless, evil, and very dangerous. . . . The Author wanted to prove that what is essential in the arts is not to be devoid of faults but rather to have beauties; that the best rules are not always the best way for avoiding the former; and that the same rules might be injurious to the latter.[35]

When one turns to Taillasson's critical writings, one finds that many of the neoclassical rules are touched upon, but none are employed in an arbitrary or axiomatic manner. In his *Observations sur quelques grands peintres*, he says of Correggio: "His color is admirable because of its truth, force, harmony, and by a certain *je ne sais quoi* of poetry. . . . Knowledge which is too profound embarrasses, stops, crushes genius, and we are never great by what we know but by what we feel. . . . Correggio is incorrect; and perhaps it would be permitted to say that his incorrectness is sometimes a beauty, since it is one of the causes of his grace."[36]

The Marquis d'Argens holds that even if rules do exist they cannot be communicated from one person to another; they cannot even be articulated: "Whoever is not born with *esprit* can never have taste; assiduous study can form a man into a savant but never into a man of taste, except when Nature has already implanted taste."[37]

Although d'Argens employs the neoclassical rules of variety, unity, harmony, and vivacity when he presents us with his reflections on Molière, Racine, Voltaire, and other writers, he contents himself with amassing *beautés* on the one side and *laideurs* on the other. His aesthetics quickly degenerates into a tedious kind of criticism.

For the most part aestheticians of the period gave the standard stock of neoclassical rules when they were pressed for examples. De Piles, in his *Diverses Conversations*, defines the "true" style as correctness of form, purity and elegance of contours, naiveté and nobility of expressions, variety, wise choice, order, and negligence of certain attributes; but, above all, a great simplicity which cuts away all superfluous ornaments, which only admits those which seem to be free of artifice, and which lets Nature always be his Mistress and makes her seem nobler, greater, and more majestic.[38]

Montesquieu invokes the same principles but joins his exposition of them to that ancient theme in Western philosophy—the great chain of being:

Our soul is made for thinking, that is to say, for perceiving, and, therefore, such a being ought to have curiosity; for, as all things are in a chain in which each idea is preceded by another and followed by another, one cannot like to see one thing without wanting to see another of them. . . . Thus, when someone shows us a part of a painting, we desire to see the part which is hidden from our view in proportion to the pleasure which the part already seen gives us.[39]

According to Montesquieu aesthetic rules are discoverable by scientific research. "It is, therefore, the pleasure which an object gives us that draws us toward another object."[40] There are five principles of pleasure: (1) curiosity, which is the most important because the mind is constantly in need of recreation or of following the various chains of things; (2) variety, which must not be too pronounced, "Gothic architecture appeared too varied, and the confusion of ornaments fatigued by their smallness";[41] (3) order, which cannot be too strong, for a Gothic building "was a species of enigma for the eye which saw it, and the soul was confused as it is when one presents it with an obscure poem";[42] (4) symmetry, which must be nicely related to variety; and (5) contrast, which must not be too pronounced as it is, according to Montesquieu, in St. Augustine's style, "St. Augustine and other writers of the *basse latinité*[43] . . . have this perpetual contrast and this *recherché* opposition."[44] But, as he explains at great length in *Esprit des lois*, the principles of pleasure vary in accordance with the climate, the customs, the institutions, and the particular sensibilities of the various races. The same opera might send an Italian audience into rapture though it leaves an English audience cool and unmoved.

> It is the same thing with pain; it is excited in us by the tearing of certain fibers of our body. The Author of nature has established that this pain be strong in proportion as the derangement of the body is great, for it is evident that the big bodies and gross fibers of the peoples of the North are less capable of being deranged than the delicate fibers of the peoples of the warm countries; the soul is there more sensitive to pain. One has to disembowel a Moscovite in order to give him a feeling.[45]

We observed in the previous chapter that Dubos believed judgements based on the sentiments are more just than those based on the rules. But as in the other parts of his aesthetics, Dubos's position in regard to the rules is equivocal. First he holds that the standard neoclassical rules are not sufficient criteria for aesthetic excellence though they might be necessary criteria: "The sublime in poetry and in painting is to touch and to please; . . . a poem, as well as a painting, would not be capable of this effect if it had no other merit than of regularity and elegance of execution."[46]

Earlier in this chapter I divided rules into two classes, those for artists and those for critics. In regard to the former Dubos holds that artists naturally observe them, if they have genius and spontaneity. Such rules, however, cannot be taught; one is born with them or not.

> They [artists] have observed the rules in order to take hold over our minds by a verisimilitude which is never belied, and a verisimilitude which is capable of making our heart believe in a fiction. . . . One does not acquire the disposition of mind of which I am speaking; one never has it if one was not born with it.[47]

One difficulty—for there are obviously many—in regard to Dubos's position is that if the rules involve verisimilitude, one would expect that they could be taught. A painting or a poem which is said to have verisimilitude is one which represents accurately something exterior to it. Verisimilitude is a species of accurate reporting or veracious description. If there is one end which education sets for itself it is surely that of teaching persons how to report upon something with accuracy in observation. And one does not always fail in this enterprise. Consequently, Dubos's position must be either false, for artistic verisimilitude, like other forms of accurate description, can be taught, or it must be true of all human activities. But in that case his position is of no great moment, because it would come to no more than, "If you do not have the facility for some art or craft, you do not have it." I suspect that the latter interpretation is Dubos's meaning, for he says that the genius required for painting and poetry is not peculiar. All the "trades" [métiers] require genius of those who practice them. Secondly, this interpretation is further supported by Dubos's way of describing the rules of poetry. Sometimes he seems to use "rules of" synonomously with "facility for," but sometimes he uses the former term as if he were talking about the "tools of the trade," or the hints, pointers, and "rules of thumb" which can be taught:

> As for the poets, the principles of the practice of their art are so easy to understand and to put into practice that one does not even need a master to help one study

them. A man born with genius can teach himself all the rules of French prosody during the space of two months.[48]

Such rules, so Dubos sometimes holds, are not even necessary for aesthetic excellence: "A work can be bad without there being any breach of the rules, just as a work full of faults according to the rules can be excellent."[49]

He modifies this position a few pages on; it appears that if all aesthetic rules were broken, then the work could not have any aesthetic value. But no particular rule is either necessary or sufficient for aesthetic worth, "It is nonetheless true that if in a work all the essential rules were violated the work could not please."[50]

As for the rules for the critic or the amateur, Dubos's position is unequivocal. The amateur, or the ordinary man who has a liking for the fine arts and is conversant with them, has no need of the rules; he judges by sentiment. The critic is a sort of deceitful or interested intermediary who places himself between the amateur and the work of art. The critic delivers himself of oracular conundrums and priestly incantations. The artists assume the same role when they try to defend or explain their work:

New works are at first appreciated by the judges—the men of the cloth and the public—in quite a different manner. Such works would quickly be appreciated justly if the public were as capable of defending its sentiment and making it known as it is capable of making a decision. But the public has a tendency to let itself be troubled by the persons whose profession it is to make such works.[51]

The public does not "make a mistake, because it judges of the matter with disinterest [*désintéressement*] and because it judges by sentiment."[52]   Dubos takes Pascal to task for saying that persons must know the rules in order to judge:

> Pascal had not adequately reflected upon the matter when he wrote that those who judge of a work of art by the rules are comparable to persons who tell the time by means of a watch while those who do not know the rules are like those who have none.[53]

Dubos is decidedly democratic:

> All men, by means of their interior sentiment, know without knowing [connoissent sans sçavoir] the rules, and whether a production of the fine arts is good or bad, and whether the reasonings that they hear are spurious or not . . . the groundlings, without knowing the rules, judge as capably of a play as the men of the profession.[54]

What is this "knowing without knowing" [connaître sans savoir]?   Dubos does not content himself with a paradox nor with the Pascalian banality of "The heart has its reasons which the mind does not understand."   Dubos attempts to give an analysis of "being acquainted with . . . but not knowing" which I find subtle and helpful.

The first step in his analysis is to assert that aesthetic knowing without knowing is noninferential; that is, no rules are employed, and no rules could even be given after the judgment.

> One recognizes that the poet has chosen a touching subject and that he has imitated it well, just as one recognizes without reasoning whether the painter has painted a beautiful person or whether someone who has done the portrait of our friend has captured the resemblance. Is it necessary, to judge whether the portrait resembles or not, to take the proportions of the face of our friend and compare them to the proportions of the portrait?[55]

Obviously not. One apprehends the resemblance immediately, or if one does have hesitations, one gradually sees the resemblance by looking more closely, or from a different angle, or perhaps interpreting the expression of the mouth or of the eyes. In any case, one does not begin with mathematical measurements. One would not conclude that a certain painting is a portrait of our friend by such measurements. What is essential is to be able to see and appreciate the resemblance. Rules would be of no help.

The second step is to describe the kind of knowledge that the amateur has. It is the result of long experience with a certain subject. It involves an adroitness and a facility that cannot be learned as one learns geometric principles, step by step, proposition by proposition. Aesthetic knowledgeability can only be acquired by practicing and engaging oneself in the arts:

> If there is one art that depends upon the speculations of philosophers, it is that of navigation on the high seas. Let someone ask the navigators whether the old pilots who have only their experience, or if one wishes, their *routine* for all their knowledge—whether such old pilots would not divine better how to pilot the vessel in unknown waters than mathematicians who are new to the sea. . . . If there is anything in the presence of which reason should keep its silence when in company of experience, it is surely the question of whether a certain poem has or does not have merit.[56]

Dubos admits that "when a work treats of the sciences which are purely speculative, the merit of the work is not decided by sentiment."[57] But when it is a question of the worth of a certain painting or poem, then the rules "are so vague that one can equally maintain that the poet employed them and that he did not employ them."[58] One can rely only upon educated and well-honed experience like that of a good surgeon.

He is aware that his position might sound paradoxical. " 'What?' someone will say to me. 'Is it the case that the more one is ignorant in poetry and painting, the more one is in the state to be a good judge of poems and paintings? What a paradox!' "[59] But though Dubos is an aesthetic democrat, he does not want to be taken for an egalitarian:

> I do not include the low people among the public who are capable of pronouncing on paintings and poems, or to decide what degree of excellence they possess. The word "public" includes here only those persons who have acquired a certain illumination, either by reading or by commerce with the world; . . . works, before being judged, remain, so to speak, on the desk; . . . the public does not pronounce upon them in regard to their true merit in one single blow.[60]

Rules, moreover, are of almost no help to the public:

> The more men advance in age and the more their reason is perfected, the less faith they have in philosophical reasonings and the more confidence in sentiment and in practice. . . . Is it decided by anything other than by sentiment whether certain colors are naturally more gay than others? Those who pretend to explain this truth by principles present us with obscurities which few persons are capable of believing.[61]

He has a decided mistrust of critics and interpretations, "Thus men of the profession judge badly in general, though their reasonings examined in particular are often rather just, but they employ reasoning for a subject for which it was not made."[62]

To conclude this discussion of Dubos, one should notice that he falls into the camp which I called "aesthetic optimists."

His reasons for saying that the fine arts progress and improve are charming and quaint but patently spurious, "Our painters presently know the nature of trees and of animals more perfectly and beautifully than that which was known to the fore-runners of Raphael and to Raphael himself."[63] Since the sciences progress, and since art is an imitation of nature, Dubos concludes that the fine arts must progress as well.

Trublet follows Dubos in many respects. In the third volume of his *Essais* (1754), he asserts:

> We owe the rules to the first works, and [we owe] the first works to genius alone. We owe the second works in part to the first, in part to the rules, but to a large extent to genius. . . . An ordinary man might make a work that conforms to the rules. A great man makes a work which gives rise to new rules. The first grafts were taken from trees that had never been grafted. In the same way there are works of genius that had no models but have served as models for other works.[64]

We notice the same tendency that we encountered in Batteux to particularize aesthetic rules to the point of their ceasing to be rules:

> Most of the rules are good. It is less a question of reforming them than of continually adding new ones, in proportion as one makes more reflections on good works of art, and as there appear new works for new reflections. Every excellent work should add to art, and in this manner art becomes more perfect.[65]

Although Trublet shares Dubos's aesthetic optimism, he gives it a better foundation. The arts progress at least technically. One can produce more varied and purer tones on the piano than on the clavier, for example. But he does not assert, as Dubos does, that technical progress implies aesthetic progress in the fine arts. And it is well that he does not do so.

Crousaz has little to say about rules and spontaneity. As one would expect, he makes the typical bow to the neoclassical principle of "unity in variety," which had been repeated for centuries, and which applies as readily to a wheelbarrow as to a piano concerto of Mozart. He hybridizes neoclassicism with utilitarianism. Objects tend to have aesthetic value in proportion as all of their parts are related to a single end. He compares the human body with works of art, but, if one takes the comparison seriously, one would have to ask what the purpose of the human body was. One can readily assign purposes to objects like umbrellas, tweezers, lampshades, and so on. But when one applies the notion of finalism to man, one is left speechless, or one must reply in terms of "man considered as so-and-so." For example, a man might be considered to have a certain religious destiny, or particular men might be said to have certain vocations or trades. But there is no end of man as such; one must place him in some religious or political context, or, on the other hand, consider him in the light of a particular vocation before the question can be answered. Now since the one term of comparison between successful works of art and the human machine is unclear, the answer to the question "What is the purpose of art?" hardly breaks through with clarity. But since Crousaz does not seem to take his theories of finalism and utilitarianism very seriously, there is no reason why we should either. He quickly passes over the subject to tell us that aesthetic rules are relative: "It is the same thing with beauty as it is with health. What is enough to nourish an infant would let a mature man die of hunger; . . . health and beauty are not imaginary, they are real but relative and not absolute."[66]

Crousaz concludes by telling us that if man had been differently constituted he would feel different beauties. "One imputes to the object all by itself all of the effect, though one contains in oneself a good part of the cause."[67]

André says that there are three things that one has a tendency to confound:

> The general notions of the pure mind, which gives us the eternal rules of the beautiful; the natural sentiments of the soul, where the sentiments mix themselves with purely spiritual ideas without destroying them; and the prejudices of education and of custom which sometimes seem to upset both of the former two categories.[68]

Corresponding to these three strata are three types of beauty:

> There is an essential beauty, independent of all intuition, even divine; there is a natural beauty, independent of the opinion of mankind; finally, there is a sort of beauty which is an institution of man, and which is to a certain point arbitrary.[69]

When pressed for examples, André gives us very few. Form is his example for the first sort; for the second, all things made by God; and for the third, that the column of the Tuscan order should be seven times as high as the diameter of its base, the Doric eight times, the Ionic nine, and the Corinthian ten. His chief interest seems to lie in what he calls "arbitrary beauty." He does not realize that giving so much attention to conventional or arbitrary beauty undermines the reader's belief in essential and natural beauty.

> But for greater ease, it would perhaps be necessary to divide arbitrary beauty into several species: a beauty of genius, a beauty of taste, a beauty of caprice. A beauty

of genius is not founded on an understanding of essential beauty but rather extended in order to form a particular system of application of the general rules.[70]

André does not have the boldness to admit that the eternal rules are vacuous nor the perspicacity to see that the notion of "eternal rules modified to meet unique works of art" is contradictory.

To avoid giving the impression that all aesthetic absolutists of the period were as dogmatic and dull as Madame Dacier, one should cite de Marcenay's *Essai sur la beauté*, which appeared in 1770. The book is brief, elegant, and could easily have been read through while one was waiting in an antechamber. De Marcenay wants to give what he calls the "signs of beauty," by which I suppose he means the criteria of beauty, for he adds, "One will no longer be exposed to the caprices of a fiery and lawless imagination."[71] He quickly supplies the reader with the precepts of neoclassicism: "Beauty is founded on the justness of proportions, of which the harmonious cooperation forms a whole as perfect as possible. . . . It is this relation among the different parts of the whole, in proportion, as much because of their particular properties and their exterior forms, . . . it is this exact rapport . . . of which beauty is the result."[72]

De Marcenay maintains that for each genus there is a perfect type, which is ideal. The actual instances of the genus are only approximations. He writes as if there were an aesthetic great chain of being:

One could establish for each mode a scale of proportion between the possible beauty and its contrary. . . . Thus, therefore, supposing that this scale has a thousand degrees (although one cannot assign limits to the power of the supreme Being), the beauty of each mode would begin at the middle and mount gradually to the thousandth

degree; . . . beauty is the degree of perfection assigned
to these different modes . . . and cannot therefore be
arbitrary or dependent upon the caprice in regard to the
evaluation of the divers degrees.[73]

According to de Marcenay, then, all horses, for example,
that exist, have existed, or will exist are various approximations
of the archetypal horse. Secondly, the various instances of
the genus horse are arranged on a scale of rising perfection.
Transferring this theory to the fine arts, de Marcenay would
conclude that the artist tries to apprehend the ideal type of a
certain mode—perhaps a landscape or a *fête galante*—and his
actual painting is an approximation of the type.

De Marcenay holds that there exists an aristocracy of taste,
for not everyone or every society can appreciate the various
degrees of perfection of which objects are susceptible. Taste
is a part of knowledge and of civilization. A man is said to
have taste not by how he feels about an object but by what he
can discern in the object:

> It is evident, I say, that most of these nations, given
> their ignorance, are much less capable of deciding this
> question [whether or not an object has aesthetic value]
> than those which, by a continual application of the
> sciences, have improved their understanding and
> perfected the arts by the exercise of sentiment.[74]

It is the "exercise of sentiment" that leads one to perceive
the rarest quality of the arts—grace. According to de Marcenay
an object can obey all the rules and, therefore, be beautiful but
only coldly so.

> If one wants to examine works which, in spite of the
> excellence of proportions, are not accompanied by grace,

one quickly perceives that the artist was more interested in the beauty of forms than to make felt the expression of the moment.[75]

By separating the two ideas of aesthetic grace and beauty, however, de Marcenay undermines his theory of the great aesthetic chain of perfection. At the beginning of his book, he had equated degrees of perfection with degrees of beauty. But he is far too sensitive a writer not to realize that there are many paintings and poems which are perfect according to all the rules, but which are destitute of interest, of warmth, or particuliarity, or, to use his own term, "grace." In other words, the cunning *je ne sais quoi* reappears, even in the writings of such a Platonic absolutist as de Marcenay. It is the same *je ne sais quoi* that the Prince de Ligne tried to introduce into the parks of Beloeil, and the same that Marivaux has appear and say:

> I am the *je ne sais quoi* that pleases in architecture, in
> furnishings, in gardens, in everything that can be the
> object of taste. Do not search for me under a certain
> form; I have a thousand, and not one which is fixed;
> that's why one sees me without knowing me, without
> being able to seize me or define me. I am felt; one
> cannot lay one's hands on me.[76]

I shall conclude this chapter, as I did the last, with a discussion of Diderot. Earlier in the present chapter I divided the aestheticians of the period into two main groups: those who held that aesthetic rules are absolute, and those who held that such rules are relative. The defining trait of the latter group, as we saw, was that there exists no way of adjudicating aesthetic disagreements. One might cudgel one's opponent, fulminate against him, refuse to admit him ever again into one's salon; but there is no rational way of refuting him. Although there are many varieties of aesthetic absolutism and of relativism, as we have seen, the two groups are logically exhaustive. He whom I have called an *aesthetic antiquarian*, as exemplified by Madame Dacier, must, as we have seen, give up his ground for absolutism, although he still clings to the belief that Greek and Roman artists codified the eternal laws of the arts. Diderot, however, tries to hybridize certain tenets of the two positions. Since they are logically incompatible, his attempt is doomed to failure. The best way to describe his position is to call him a relativist in regard to aesthetic rules, although he believed he had shown how to adjudicate aesthetic disagreements. Before discussing his attempt, let us note certain of his statements about aesthetic rules in general.

First, although Diderot is not consistent in his position concerning relationships, he holds that the feeling of beauty is both logically and temporally prior to aesthetic rules and judgement:

> The feeling of beauty is the result of a long series of
> observations; and these observations, when does one
> make them? At every point in time. These are obser-
> vations which dispense with analysis. Taste has
> pronounced a long time before knowing the motive of
> its judgement. Taste sometimes searches without finding
> the motive, and, nonetheless, taste persists.[77]

Aesthetic rules exist to help chiefly the aesthetically feeble —those who have no taste, or very little, and those who are just becoming acquainted with the fine arts. Diderot holds that rules are of great help to them and also to nations that are slipping into decadence. But genius is spontaneous; it has no need of rules: "The rules have made of art a routine, and I do not know whether they have been more helpful than useful. Let us put it squarely: the rules have helped the ordinary man; they have injured the man of genius."[78]

According to Diderot, there is a great abyss between taste

and genius. The former reflects, proceeds by the laws, and produces works of little note. The latter is spontaneous, independent of the laws, and erects the models for other artists to follow. Even the rules of Aristotle—which writers in the seventeenth and eighteenth centuries took far more literally than Aristotle intended—are not absolute:

> I beg Aristotle's pardon, but it is a vicious sort of criticism to deduce exclusive rules from the most perfect works, as if the means of pleasing were not infinite. Genius can infringe almost any of these laws with success. It is true that the troupe of slaves, while admiring, cry sacrilege.[79]

What the one unbreachable law is Diderot never quite makes clear, but it seems to be something as vague as "Never fail to imitate the eternal beauties of nature or to express the profoundest sentiments of the human heart."

> If the observation of nature is not the dominant taste of the writer or of the artist, do not expect anything of value; and should you recognize this taste from his earliest years, suspend your judgement even so, for the muses are women, and they do not accord their favors to those who solicit them most ardently. . . . Every composition worthy of praise is in every respect in accord with nature; one must be able to say, "I have not seen this phenomenon, but it exists."[80]

Diderot has nothing but scorn for those who apply the so-called rules with absolutist rigor and critics who try to interpose themselves between the work of art and the amateur, "What a stupid occupation it is to try ceaselessly to keep us from feeling pleasure, or to make us blush because of the pleasure we have taken in something—that is the occupation of the critic."[81]

It is only to be expected that Diderot nods approvingly at the neoclassical rules of symmetry, harmony, and balance, but he does not hold that they are necessary and sufficient conditions of beauty. Genius can break them with impunity.

Let us now turn to the way in which Diderot tries to reconcile his version of relativism with absolutism. He asserts:

> However it might be with all the causes of diversity in our judgements, it is not a reason for saying that the *beau réel*, that which consists in the perception of relations, is a chimera; the application of this principle might vary infinitely, and its accidental modification occasions various treatises and literary wars, but the principle is, nonetheless, constant.[82]

The "principle" is that the perception of beauty consists in the perception of relationships, either within an object considered by itself or between one object and others. Even though men do, as a matter of fact, vary in their perceptions of beauty ("There are perhaps no two men on earth who perceive exactly the same relations in an object"),[83] ideally men should agree because the relationships exist independently of men's thoughts or feelings about them. Diderot's theory is that if the conditions which he specifies are met, then men ought to agree about the aesthetic worth of a given object. Let us first see what the conditions are and then try to determine in what sense men *ought* to agree if the conditions are met.

Diderot tries to define the term *bon esprit* without circularity. A *bon esprit* is one who correctly perceives the relations which are the foundations of aesthetic beauty, "We admit only those relations among beautiful objects which a *bon esprit* can seize upon distinctly and with readiness."[84]

The *bon esprit* is (1) one who has a great deal of experience of the fine arts and is, therefore, most sensitive to the *rapports*; (2) one who is without personal commitments, prejudices, passions, and divisive habits or customs; (3) one who has a complete understanding of the artist's medium and the development and history of the fine arts; (4) one who has clear and precise ideas about nonaesthetic matters, for nonaesthetic beliefs can influence one's aesthetic beliefs; (5) one who is free of linguistic confusions and the maladies of semantics; (6) one who has experienced the object under ideal conditions; (7) one who does not confuse his aesthetic approval or disapproval with his sensual liking or disliking; and (8) one who has considered the object disinterestedly and with critical acumen.[85]

Diderot's version of objective relativism fails because one might reasonably ask the following question: "Here are two men who fulfill your eight criteria, and so, according to your theory, they ought to agree. But as a matter of fact, they do not. Why?"

In what sense should we interpret Diderot's "ought to agree"? That it is empirically to be expected that they will agree? However it sometimes occurs that two persons who fulfill Diderot's criteria do not agree. At this point Diderot might say that the two persons do not really fit the criteria. But then one has started down the insidious path of banishing data and rearranging appearances. Secondly, if "ought to agree" is to be taken in the logical sense, then the notion of the *bon esprit* would have to include the notion of "perceiving the real relations of objects." But then Diderot would be arguing in a circle, for he was attempting to show the criteria of "perceiving the real relations of objects." Thirdly, if the "ought" is neither empirical nor analytic, it must have the force of "It is greatly to be hoped and advised that persons who fulfill the eight criteria do agree." But what would be the point of such a hope or of such a piece of advice? In matters of statecraft and diplomacy, in matters of ethics and politics, the plea for uniformity of opinion is often important. The diplomatic corps might dedicate itself to certain principles, or the people might uphold certain ideals; but then it is a question of interest and economy of action. However, the uniformity of aesthetic judgement of all men constituted like the man of *bon esprit* is not related to action and is to the interest of no one—except to Diderot who is trying to rescue his system from anarchy. The uniformity of taste would be as tedious as if everyone had the same face; it would lead to bleak and grayish homogeneity of the arts.

I shall now leave the second dominant theme of eighteenth-century French aesthetics and move on to the third. Since the third theme is closely related to the second, it is only with a certain violence to the subject that I do so. I can only hope that what my exposition loses because of this categorization of ideas, it gains by way of clarity.

III Imitation and Creation

THE title of the present chapter might lead the reader to believe that the French aestheticians of the Enlightenment neatly arranged themselves into two hostile camps: those who held that the artist does or ought to imitate nature, and those who held that the artist does or can create something original and unprecedented. Although there are a few writers of the period who kept strictly to the one side or the other, the majority mingled on the field between the two camps. Having befriended each other, they tried to see each other's point of view and effect some kind of pact or reconciliation. As with all reconciliations, the first step was to make certain that both sides understood what the terms in question meant. As Trublet mentions in the third volume of his *Essais*:

> The proposition that art is an imitation of nature needs
> to be modified and explained in order to be understood
> in its true sense. One generally gives the proposition too
> wide a latitude. The beauties of art and of nature
> are of different orders.[1]

Although one might correctly call an artifact or an object in nature "beautiful," according to Trublet, different criteria are used. One demands symmetry and regularity of works of art;

93

one rarely, if ever, finds these qualities in nature. Trublet shared the common feeling of distrust in and dislike of unveiled nature that many of his contemporaries felt. Without the help of man, nature violated all aesthetic principles. Nevertheless, certain persons in England were beginning to use the language of aesthetic approval and discrimination in regard to nature, and the vogue later spread to France. Once again the aestheticians of the period found themselves in a dualistic bind, this time between art and reality, or imitation and creation. Such questions as the following assumed great importance:

1. Does the artist simply copy the beauties of nature, or should he select? And if he should, according to what principles?

2. If the artist does not simply imitate the beauties of nature, does he invent or create certain beauties himself without the aid of the senses? And if he does so, how is this creative process to be explained?

3. How closely should the artist imitate nature? In the manner of the naturalist? Or should he idealize nature? Or should he try to give a gentle satire or mime of nature?

4. How can one explain imitating the ugly, or the painful, things in nature if the chief principle of art is to please?

Let us see in detail how these questions were answered by the writers whom we are discussing. We shall begin with a sure point of orthodoxy, Batteux. As we have seen, according to Batteux, one of the chief ends of art is to imitate *la belle nature*. To imitate, he holds, is to copy a model. Therefore one needs a prototype which has the traits that one wants to imitate, and the copy which represents it. Nature is defined as everything which exists, or everything which is readily conceivable. The artist selects from among the richness of nature.

Batteux, however, shortly loses his way in the thicket of his arguments. At one point he asserts that in an imitation one ought to see "nature, not as it is in itself, but as it could be, and as one could conceive of it by the mind."[2] The artist

94

would choose but as a connoisseur. Nature presents many tedious and stupid objects, and the artist must decide which to imitate. But at another point Batteux writes:

> To invent in the arts is not to give a being to an object but to recognize it for what it is. And the men of genius who dig deepest only discover what existed previously. They are creators only in that they have observed, and, reciprocally, they are observers only to be in a position to create.[3]

When he asks himself whether artists simply copy the beauties of nature, or whether certain artists have created something *ab ovo*, he is equally inconsistent:

> There are, therefore, happy moments for the genius when the soul, inflamed as if by a divine fire, represents to itself nature in its entirety and spreads over all objects this spirit of life which animates them. . . . This state of the soul is called "enthusiasm" . . . a celestial vision, a divine influence, a prophetic spirit.[4]

Batteux is quick to retract the virtues of enthusiasm and seems to imply that it does not really exist. It is a composite notion and reducible to simple entities which are well known. Since Batteux assumes—at least in the argument that is to follow—that there could not be any trait in a whole which is not contained in at least one of its parts, enthusiasm has no real existence. Enthusiasm is "an exquisite justness of *esprit*, a fecund imagination, and above all a heart filled with a noble fire, and which catches flame easily on the sight of certain objects."[5]

As Batteux proceeds, nature becomes more inaccessible and ideal, as the arts become more approximative and shackled. He asserts that "imitation, in order to be as perfect as possible, must have two qualities: exactitude and liberty. The one regulates imitation, and the other animates nature."[6]

A few pages on, however, it appears that only nature can combine exactitude and liberty:

> It seems that nature has reserved to herself the possibility of reconciling them [liberty and exactitude] in order to make her superiority known. She always appears naive, ingenuous. She proceeds without study and without reflection, because she is free. On the other hand the arts almost always bear the marks of their servitude.[7]

At this point the reader might wonder how I can refer to Batteux as a point of orthodoxy when his writings, as we have noticed before, are so riddled with contradictions. I think it suffices to point out that most of the world's chief orthodoxies —religious and political—contain incompatible assertions. To suppose that orthodoxy entails consistency is to set one's hopes too high.

Batteux draws the natural conclusion that judging the value of works of art involves comparing them with their originals in nature. Mere resemblance, he asserts, is not enough; one must please by the representation. To achieve aesthetic pleasure the surest means that the artist can employ is to expand the spectator's vision of the possible and to lead him to see that certain elements are natural. Batteux seems to be toying with the idea of art as microcosm; given certain elements drawn from nature, a work of art brings them together to produce new and original combinations, so that the work represents a little world which is neither a mere imitation of reality nor utterly divorced from it.

Concerning the judgements that the mind brings to bear on imitations, two sorts are possible: (1) "This work has faults." To make this kind of judgement, one has only to compare the object with its original. But according to Batteux,

(2) "This work does not have all the beauties of which it is susceptible" involves knowing the object in its entirety.

It appears, then, that the artist is passive, and that *la belle nature* already exists. The artist might emphasize or call attention to certain beauties by a judicious choice, but he cannot create a single new element. When we press Batteux for a more concise definition of *la belle nature*, as Diderot did in his *Recherchés Philosophiques sur l'origine et la nature du beau*, he tells us that it is the aspect of nature which has the closest relation to our own interests and desires, and, secondly, the aspect which is the most perfect. The arts, so it appears, simply imitate different aspects of *la belle nature*:

> Poetry exists only by imitation. It is the same thing
> with painting, dance, and music; nothing is real in their
> works, everything is imagined, painted, copied, artificial.
> It is what makes their essential character as opposed
> to nature.[8]

Before discussing how Batteux explains the imitation of the ugly and the unpleasant in objects of art, we might first turn to Dubos's position regarding imitation and then discuss both writers along with Crousaz on the same subject. Dubos informs us that since one is less moved by the imitation than by that which is imitated, the artist must choose objects and situations which have considerable force. Such objects must be close to our personal interests. According to Dubos landscape painting, for example, has little interest, because one is not greatly interested in bare and unpeopled nature. One might admire the technique, but "the most beautiful countryside, let it be by Titian or by Correggio, does not move us nearly as much as would the prospect of a hideous or charming town district."[9] Dubos was writing in 1719. The vogue of nature had not yet appeared in France.

According to Dubos artistic creation is nothing other than

the capacity to perceive and imitate in a sensuous form certain aspects of nature that had never before been noticed. Nature is an infinite treasury from which the artist can draw in accordance with the merits of his own genius:

> A man born with genius sees nature, which his art imitates, with eyes other than those of persons without genius. He discovers an infinite difference between objects which to the eyes of other persons seem to be the same, and he knows so well how to feel this difference in his imitation that the most trite object becomes a new subject under his paintbrush or his pen.[10]

The artist is simply a more acute observer of human nature than the general run of humanity. He has a sharper appreciation of shades of color, nuances of words and meanings or of tones and pitch. While Batteux describes the artist's profession as one of simplifying nature and trying to embody the ideal form, Dubos maintains that the artist must be interested only in the particular and try to present the individual with the most minute traits. Almost no object is indifferent to the artist, as long as it presents a clear individuality:

> All men seem to be the same to persons of limited understanding. Men seem different from one another to persons of a wider understanding, but men are all particular and individual beings to the poet born with the genius of comedy.[11]

A good fifty years before Lessing's *The Laocoon*, Dubos introduced the distinction between poetry and painting based on the difference between time and space: "The poet can employ several traits to express the passion and the sentiment of one of his characters. . . . It is not the same with the painter who paints one sole time for each of his characters."[12] The parallelism of poetry and painting was a heated question during the eighteenth century.[13]   But to base the distinction between the two arts on time and space is not to advance very far.   For, although in an obvious sense paintings occupy space and poems take time to be read, the *personnages*, to employ Dubos's term, might be static or fluid in either art.   A static portrait is one with little or no expression, a face or a smile that allows no interpretation or leeway to the imagination.   A static character in fiction would be one that does not develop or alter.   A fluid *personnage* in a painting would be one that can be seen as embodying a number of different attitudes or expressions depending upon the way in which one looks at the object.

According to Dubos's theory the artist might better be called an investigator than an imitator.   The artist's profession is to search out and put in relief the various nuances of nature that other persons do not observe.

De la Motte has only a word or two to say about imitation. He inverses the roles of the artist and nature.   Though the artist uses the data of nature to supply the matter of his work, it is the artist who introduces the form:

> One must . . . understand by "imitation" an adroit
> imitation, that is to say, the art to make only the objects
> which are proper to produce the effect that one has pro-
> posed.   One must never separate the poet's imitation from
> his design.   It is this design which, so to speak, gives the
> law to the imitation.   It is the design which prescribes
> the true limits, and which makes the imitation good or bad
> in accordance with whether the imitation serves the
> design or not.[14]

Taillasson has little to add to the distinctions already noted. He is less interested in theories of artistic creation than in artists.   In his *Observations sur quelques grands peintres*, he asserts, "To present men with nature, no matter of what sort, and to present her to them in a new way—that is what one demands absolutely, and for this sole price does one accord a durable fame."[15]

Taillasson was, however, one of the few writers who dared to assert that art is superior to nature. In this regard he joins ranks with Voltaire and places himself against Bernardin de Saint-Pierre and, of course, Rousseau. Speaking of Michelangelo, Taillasson writes:

> To choose what is the most amiable that nature has
> produced, that which is the most grand and most noble,
> to paint the grace and the expression, to touch, to instruct,
> to elevate the soul—this is the most precious advantage
> of painting. . . . One might say that the art is, therefore,
> in some respects, superior to nature; art presents nature
> under an aspect which she rarely shows.[16]

In his poem, "Le Danger des règles dans les arts," Taillasson contrasts imitation with inspiration. It appears that though artistic creation is directed by rules, genius can break them and, in doing so, establish new rules:

> He [Jupiter] ordered that nature always be
> The sole true beauty. . . .
>
> O you whose heart is nobly agitated and who
> Burn to rise to immortality,
> Go, fly toward her, enlightened by the flame
> That the master of the Gods lighted in your soul:
> Could such a guide ever be deceitful?
>
> Placing yourself alongside of your famous rivals,
> Go and serve as a rule for your cowardly relatives.[17]

Roger de Piles, in his *Cours de peinture*, has little to say about imitation that had not already been said by other writers of the Enlightenment: "The essence and the definition of painting is the imitation of visible objects by means of form and color. It is not to be concluded, therefore, that painting strictly and faithfully imitates nature."[18]

He maintains that there are three different kinds of beauty in each branch of the fine arts: (1) *le vrai simple*, (2) *le vrai idéal*, and (3) *le vrai composé* or *le vrai parfait*. The first is faithful and strict imitation or copying. The second consists in a choice of various perfections which never combine themselves in the same manner in nature or are never found in a single model. And the third is in some way a hybrid between the first and second. I say "in some way" because it is not clear what de Piles takes himself to be describing. He says that the third kind of beauty is a composite of *le vrai simple* and *le vrai idéal*, and that it is the perfect imitation of *la belle nature*. It appears that the third sort either reduces to the second or is simply the second sort of beauty greatly expanded, for clearly (1) and (3) are incompatible, and so a hybrid beauty between them would be impossible. "It appears, then, that imitation is nothing but a choice of objects which ought to enter into the composition of the subject which the painter wants to treat."[19]

De Piles gives long inventories of the sorts of things to which the painter should pay heed once he has chosen his subject. For example, in regard to draperies, he says, "The folds should be large and few in number, as much as this is possible; this maxim being one of the things which contributes more to what one calls 'the grand manner'."[20]

We have observed that the theorists of the French Enlightenment were chiefly aesthetic hedonists though sometimes with a utilitarian bent. In the present chapter, we have noticed that many of the same writers maintained various kinds of "mimesis." It was natural, then, that a certain question should present itself to many of the aestheticians of the period: How can one explain the imitation of painful or ugly things in the fine arts? How can man take pleasure in viewing imitations of tragic events, of gruesome details, of scenes depicting massacres and panic? The question was hardly new to western thought, but three writers of the Enlightenment gave the question a new answer: Dubos, Batteux, and Crousaz.

Dubos writes:

> Every day one feels that verse and painting cause a
> sensible pleasure, but it is, nonetheless, difficult to explain
> what the pleasure consists in that often resembles
> affliction and of which the symptoms are often those of a
> profound pain. The art of poetry and the art of painting
> are never so greatly applauded as when they succeed in
> afflicting us. Generally speaking, people take more
> pleasure in crying than in laughing at the theater. . . .
> The more the actions of poetry and painting ruffle us—and
> would have made our feelings of humanity suffer had we
> directly seen the objects depicted—the more these objects
> gain hold over us. A secret charm attaches us, therefore,
> to the imitations which the poets and painters know
> how to make, at the same time during which nature
> testifies by a sort of interior shivering that something is
> going against her proper pleasure.[21]

The first part of Dubos's reply consists in pointing out that the fundamental need of man is to be occupied and that mankind loves the emotions in general. Nothing is more painful to man that a grayish insouciance or a languid apathy. If art presents imitation of strong and painful events, at least man's spirit is occupied. He is freed, at least for the moment, from the depths of melancholy and ennui. The second part of his reply refines upon the first:

> The pleasure which one feels in seeing the imitations that
> painters and poets make of objects which would have
> greatly excited us if we had encountered them in reality is

a pure pleasure. It is not followed by the inconveniences which the other serious emotions would have caused in us nor is it accompanied by them. . . .

The affliction is only, so to speak, on the surface of the heart, and we are well aware that our tears will finish at the end of the performance of the ingenious fiction which made them flow.[22]

Aesthetic sadness or "affliction," according to Dubos, differs from the afflictions one might feel during the course of ordinary life and the commerce with other human beings in the following ways: (1) If a work of art is sad or imitates some tragic and painful event, a spectator might appreciate that the work is sad or tragic, though he is in a happy or contented frame of mind. Aesthetic emotions do not banish nonaesthetic emotions. One *appreciates that* or *feels that* a work of art is sad, whereas one is *made sad by* some tragic event in the nonaesthetic world. (2) If one realizes that the work of art is a work of art, then one's symptoms of sadness—tears, sighs, or sentimental upheavals—end with the work of art. Such feelings do not linger on in the mind or leave us speechless and limp as do nonaesthetic feelings. One *remembers that* or *acknowledges that* "Phèdre" is tragic and profoundly moving, though one no longer feels such emotions. (3) One would not try to help some one through an asethetic emotion, as one often tries to help a friend through grief or dispair. If someone finds *Bérénice* and the agonies of the separation of the lovers an excruciating tragedy, one does not try to console him, give him advice, or cheer him up.

In the third part of his reply, however, Dubos tends to diminish the importance of "aesthetic afflictions," and in so doing he becomes confused:

As the impression made by imitation is not so serious as one which would go to the reason (for which there is no illusion in the sensations) and as the impression made by imitation affects only the sensitive part of the soul, the imitation is soon effaced.[23]

Dubos asserts that artistic emotions are so ephemeral and shallow that they barely touch us, or that when they do we are in the position to master and control them:

> If novels make such a long and profound impression on the souls of youth, it is because such novels awaken the emotions which they will feel in the future and are just beginning to dawn upon them. . . .
> The painter and the poet afflict as much pain upon us as we allow; . . . our souls are always master of our superficial emotions.[24]

The term "superficial emotions" is something of a bad pun, and it leads Dubos astray. Dubos calls aesthetic or artistic emotions "superficial" in one sense because they strike only the "surface" of one's soul; that is, aesthetic emotions differ from nonaesthetic in the three ways already noted. But according to other passages in his work "superficial emotions" are also those that are of little moment, unserious, and controllable. Though the first three differences that he notes between the two sorts of feelings do hold, the last does not. One would not want to say that artistic emotions are less serious or less important than nonartistic, for the two are so different that the question of comparing the two in regard to importance is idle. One is left prey to whatever the composer has written or the novelist described; one cannot control artistic emotions. We are to a large extent passive and in the hands of a force stronger than ourselves. In an obvious sense, of course, one can "control" one's artistic emotions by closing the novel, leaving the concert hall, or putting the painting in the attic. But this is less a control of one's emotions than a denial of them.

Batteux's answer to the question is far more traditional, and much less interesting, than that given by Dubos. Batteux does little more than repeat the sentiment expressed by Lucretius in *De Rerum Natura*. Batteux asserts, "It is in this that the arts have succeeded: in presenting us with an object that frightens us and at the same time showing us that it is a question of art in order to give by this means the pleasure of the emotion without any disagreeable mixture."[25]

According to Batteux, we enjoy the imitation of terrifying and hideous things in nature because we know that we are in safety. Though he admits that this is not the only reason for our pleasure, he gives us no other and lets the matter rest.[26]

Crousaz does not attempt to give an analysis of artistic feelings, as does Dubos, nor does he give a traditional answer, as does Batteux. Crousaz simply applies the tenets of neoclassicism. Ugly things in nature can be beautiful in imitations (he mentions a painting of a spider, of a monster, of a murder) because "the mind enjoys discovering uniformity amid this great diversity. . . . One enjoys letting one's mind linger on variety without order, without connections, without uniformity, in order to become more sensible to proportion when one discovers it."[27] The importance of the ugly is therefore therapeutic.

"Beauties," according to Crousaz, are synonomous with "regularities." One should not be "surprised that what is beautiful to one person is not so to another; that does not prove that beauty is imaginary; one should simply conclude that beauty is hidden and difficult."[28] Crousaz assumes that to become well acquainted with a subject one should become acquainted with its contrary. There is evidently a confusion in Crousaz's thought. Although it is true that to become knowledgeable about opera, for example, involves subjecting oneself to bad performances as well as good, the contrast in this case is between "opera done well" and "opera done badly." Now if Crousaz is attempting to apply the same sort of argument to all the fine arts, he should say that it is well to be acquainted with

105

bad performances, poor novels, inferior paintings, and so on, in order to develop connoisseurship. However, if imitations of the ugly can be beautiful, as he asserts, then there is no reason to suppose that our acquaintance with such imitations will help us to appreciate imitations of "beauties." The problem was soon to be "solved" by introducing the notions of the *pittoresque* and the *sublime*.

Let us now examine Diderot's position concerning the limitation of painful and repugnant objects in art. One should notice first of all that Diderot differs greatly from Dubos concerning the importance and tone of artistic emotions. For Dubos they were shallow and controllable; for Diderot they are profound and often overwhelming. In his *Essai sur la peinture*, Diderot writes:

> If taste were a thing of caprice, if there were no rule concerning the beautiful, where would these emotions come from—these delicious emotions that arise so suddenly, so involuntarily, so tumultuously from the depths of our soul, these emotions which enlarge or constrict us, and which force our eyes to shed tears of joy, of sadness, of admiration, either in seeing some great physical phenomenon or from the recounting of some great moral trait? Sophistry, you will never persuade my heart that it is mistaken to shudder, or my viscera that they are mistaken to be greatly moved.[29]

After establishing the seriousness and power of artistic emotions, Diderot, in the same work, asserts that taste is an accumulation of forgotten impressions and emotions, all of which are spontaneously brought to bear on an object newly presented to the mind. "What is taste? An acquired facility by reiterated experiences which seizes the true or the good with the circumstance that renders it beautiful and is promptly and incisively touched by it."[30]

Diderot is quick to add that taste is not infallible, but that

> reason rectifies sometimes the rapid judgment of sensibility; it calls it to task. Because of that there are so many productions forgotten almost as soon as they are applauded, and so many others either unnoticed or disdained that receive, in due time, because of the progress of the mind and art, a closer attention and the tribute that they merited.[31]

In the *Salon de 1767* Diderot asks himself why he feels pleasure when he cries. How can he reconcile his enjoyment of certain paintings which imitate or represent painful subjects with his realization that such subjects are actually unpleasant? It appears that Diderot implicitly assumes the truth of Aristotle's doctrine of pleasure and pain; men are naturally attracted by pleasurable objects, or at least by those that they believe to be so, and are repelled by painful objects. How, then, can rational human beings naturally be attracted to imitations of painful or disastrous objects in nature? As it is so often the case with Diderot, the reader is presented with a large assortment of explanations, many of which are incompatible with others. His first reply is based on La Rochefoucauld's maxim to the effect that one takes a certain pleasure in the adversities of one's greatest friends or, at least, not a distinct displeasure. Because of our natural egoism we congratulate ourselves upon not being in a similar unhappy state and, thus, not subjected to the same horrors or torments.

A more mature consideration of the same problem soon follows in the same *Salon*. Diderot, two hundred years before Edward Bullough's celebrated essay on "Psychical Distance," sketches a similar theory to explain our enjoyment of the tragic. Just as there is an actual physical point which is most advantageous for seeing a certain painting (depending on its size, the lighting of the room, the vision of the spectator), so, too, there is a natural point at which imitations of the tragic and painful are sufficiently removed from the personal interests of the spectator so that he is not injured or threatened. One has the illusion of witnessing terrifying events, and one is in a sense "terrified." At the same time, given the proper distance, one is aware that it is only an illusion, and consequently one has feelings of security. If the illusion is too crude or too close to the spectator's interests or personal state, then the illusion is broken because of an excess of realism. Art loses its illusion, and reality intrudes upon us. On the contrary, however, if the illusion is too great, that is, the objects imitated or represented are so greatly removed from the interests of the spectator that the illusion of art dissipates into haziness and dreams, then the mind shortly loses interest.

If we construe Diderot's theory as a psychological one, it would be supported or refuted by experience. He is attempting to correlate two events: (1) certain feelings of aesthetic enjoyment, and (2) certain imitations or representations of objects that are intrinsically painful or repugnant. When certain conditions are met, for example, that the object (a) is not related by painful memories or associations to the spectator, (b) is not too close to reality, or (c) is not too far removed from human desires and interests, then, so Diderot appears to hold, one can take artistic delight in imitations of the ugly or terrifying. As long as his theory is given a psychological interpretation, one would have no formal complaints about it. If that is how human beings sometimes react, then that is how they react. But if the theory were a philosophical explication of our taking pleasure in the tragic, then it would be circular. If one asks, "At what point can one take pleasure?" Diderot could only reply, "When the object is neither too close to your personal desires and feeling nor too far removed from them." If we press him for an interpretation of "neither too close to . . . nor too far removed from," he would have little else to reply than, "When one feels aesthetic pleasure." But since Diderot's theory, or rather his sketch of the theory, seems to be psychlogical in tone, it seems to escape the criticism that I have just mentioned.

I should now like to examine Diderot's theories concerning the role of limitation and the role of the artist. But as a prelude to this examination, it might not be inadvisable to pause for a moment to make a slight reflection. When dealing with certain philosophers like Diderot, it is very much like dealing with women; if one forces them to be consistent, they not only lose their charm but also the sharpness of their intuitions. When all is said and done, consistency is not such a precious quality that all others should be sacrificed to it. There are consistent bores and consistent pedants. Consistency has become an *idée fixe* among many analytic philosophers of the twentieth century. Although it is an important requirement, it is, nevertheless, one which forces us to leave many persons waiting in the antechamber, without ever receiving them into the salon: philosophers who are volatile rather than strict, perceptive rather than probing, and who write with an irregular brilliance rather than a consistent flame.

There are, I find, two chief antinomies in Diderot's thought concerning imitation and creation. I call them "antinomies" because the logical form of his difficulties resembles the form of the famous antinomies in Kant's *The Critique of Pure Reason* and *The Critique of Judgement*. Other persons writing on Diderot's aesthetics might prefer to dismiss his philosophical difficulties as "contradictions" and consider the matter finished. Although antinomies might be a species of contradiction, they are, to speak loosely, attractive contradictions. Antinomies are seductive. In an antinomy in general, one is first presented with two propositions which seem to be incompatible—in many or all of the senses of "incompatible." Secondly, a third proposition is introduced which is supposed to assuage the inincompatibility and rectify the matter. And lastly, various corollaries are drawn from the set of three propositions. It should be understood that I am in no way attempting to make a Kantian out of Diderot. I am simply trying to make clear certain important parts of Diderot's aesthetics by using a way of philosophical presentation often employed by Kant.

Antinomy 1: Diderot's fondness for natural beauty and sublimity is too well known to need support from the texts. In his *De la poésie dramatique*, for example, he tells us that

> water, air, earth, fire—everything is good in nature; even
> the storms that rise toward the end of autumn and
> shake the trees, break them, tear off the dead branches—
> everything is good in nature, even the tempests that make
> the oceans swell, and volcanoes—everything in nature
> seems to have a purpose, to be part of an immense
> economy, and, therefore, is beautiful.[32]

He tells us in the *Essais sur la peinture* that nature does nothing incorrectly, that every form, whether beautiful or ugly, has its cause. He asserts that there is no object in nature which is not as it should be. Nature, considered in its entirety, is perfect. Opposed to this sentiment, however, one finds the following:

> There are arid spaces in nature, and there must not be
> any in art. Sometimes nature is dry, and art must never
> be so.[33]

Elsewhere one finds Diderot acknowledging imperfections in nature—hunchbacks, hideously gnarled trees, deformed animals, and, what is even more important, the great wastes and uniformities of nature. It is at this point that Diderot tries to reconcile these two opinions; he turns to the well-worn notion of the endless chain of nature. If one considers nature in its entirety, one sees that there are neither lapses nor lacunae. If one encounters a certain deformity, it occupies a certain link in creation and is preceded by gradations, often minute, of other deformities. As Diderot asserts:

> We say of a man that we see passing in the street that he
> is deformed. Yes, but this is only in accordance with
> our poor rules. We say of a statue that its proportions are
> perfect. Yes, but only according to our rules. But what
> if we consider the object from the point of view of
> nature's rules?[34]

In the first antinomy Diderot wants to hold that nature is perfect in its entirety, so that the artist will have a perfect model.
Yet he also wants to affirm the existence of the ugly and imperfect. The only solution, so he argues, is to say that the artist
glimpses only certain links in the chain of being; the artist sees
only part of nature, and so he applies human logic to the infinite perfection of nature. Often the artist produces monsters
worse than any in nature.

To illustrate this theory, Diderot asks us to suppose that
nature is personified, and that we place her in front of the
statue of *Antinoüs* or of the *Venus of Medici*. Let us suppose
that the statue is covered with a veil so that only the extreme
portion of one of the feet is allowed to show. And now one
asks Nature to complete the statue in accordance with the portion which is visible. Unfortunately, working in accordance
with the necessity of her own laws, instead of producing a work
of art, an object worthy of our admiration, Nature would exe-
cute a mutilated figure or something deformed. Once a mole-
cule is given, everything is determined for Nature. The force
of a small modification which completely changes and determines everything for Nature does not affect us. We do not
know the effect of the part upon the whole. Art is always imperfect, so Diderot concludes, and our admiration is always
limited. Our attention can only focus itself upon the isolated
and fragmented.

From the resolution of the first antinomy flows a number of
corollaries. I say *flow* rather than *follow* because the three
propositions of the antinomy do not entail the corollaries that
Diderot draws but, nonetheless, make them understandable and

weakly coherent. First, although imitation of nature is the only possible object of the true artist, he can only approximate, hint at, and attempt to be as true to nature as possible. Secondly, nature is vastly superior to art and is the heaven of invention which the artist can never attain but must always yearn after. He tells us in his *Pensées Détachées sur la peinture* that the harmony of the most beautiful painting is only a feeble imitation of the harmony in nature. The colors of the artist can never equal those of nature in vivacity or in depth. The artist is forced to make a sort of great chain of his own, in which his own colors are midway between the perfect colors of nature and the base colors of the technically incompetent artist.

Antinomy 2: The second chief antinomy concerns the role of the artist in relation to nature. To appreciate the first side of the antinomy, it will be best to translate at length a passage from Diderot's *Recherchés Philosphiques*:

> What does one mean when one says to an artist, "Imitate *la belle nature?*" Either one does not know what one is commanding, or one says to him: "If you have a flower to paint, and if it is indifferent which one you paint, take the most beautiful of all flowers; if you have a plant to paint, and if your subject does not require that it be an oak or an elm—dry, broken, branchless—take the most beautiful plant. In general, if you have an object to paint from nature, and if it is indifferent which one you are to choose, take the most beautiful."
>
> From which it follows: (1) that the imitation of beautiful nature demands the most wide and profound study of the productions of every sort; (2) that when one has the most perfect understanding of nature, and of the limits placed for each production, it would not be less true that the number of occasions on which the most beautiful would be employed in the arts of imitation would be to the number of occasions on which it is necessary

to prefer the less beautiful, as unity is to infinity; (3) that
though there is in effect a maximum of beauty in each
object of nature, considered by itself . . . there is not, however, either beauty or ugliness in the productions
considered relatively to the use that one makes of them
in the arts of imitation.[35]

It appears, then, that the artist is to select beautiful parts
of nature for imitation, and that he is to proceed by an ideal
model. At certain points in his exposition, Diderot seems to
hold that art is a method for attaining the ideal beauty. The
artist is not to imitate nature closely but to try to achieve the
ideal model. In the *Paradoxe sur le comédien,* Diderot tells us
that it is not permitted to imitate nature, even *la belle nature.*
One must never imitate nature too closely. But on the other
side of the antinomy, we are presented with a proposition
which seems to wreck the notion of imitation:

Whether I think or do not think of the façade of the Louvre,
all the parts which compose it have the same relationships
between them and the same arrangement; whether there
were men or not, it would not be less beautiful, but only
for persons constituted as we are, with a mind and a
body.[36]

If this is true, there is no *belle nature* unless there exist human
beings, and not just any human beings, but those that have the
bon sens, as described in the preceding chapter of the present
work. It appears that according to Diderot beauty exists only
in the artist's imitation of nature, not in nature itself. Artistic
as well as natural beauty is a hybrid of man's sensibility and
the data of nature.

How does Diderot resolve the second antinomy? How can
the artist have as his sole end the imitation of *la belle nature*
when beauty does not objectively exist in nature? Diderot

seems to be using the word "imitation" equivocally. The artist can imitate nature directly in that sense he is a copyist. Diderot's scorn for the portraitist who does not interpret his subject is well known. The artist, however, can also imitate the idea that he has of nature, that is, the hybrid of natural data and his own sensibility. The true poet and the true artist, as opposed to the poetaster and the copyist, do not copy nature as it is given to unaided sensibility but imitate the reflection of nature made upon their own imagination. The artist is not to imitate relationships that are purely intellectual or scientific but only those that touch or move the subject.

That Diderot is struggling in the second antinomy between neoclassical orthodoxy and the new wave of expressionistic romanticism is made all the more evident by the corollaries that flow from his "resolution" of the second antinomy. In the *Salon de 1767* he tells us that the artist creates nothing but only imitates, composes, combines, exaggerates, enlarges upon, and diminishes various parts of nature. In the *Essais sur la peinture*, Diderot writes:

> Michelangelo gave the most perfect form possible to the
> dome of St. Peter's. . . . What was it that inspired this
> curve rather than an infinity of others that he might
> have chosen? Day-to-day experience of life. It is that
> which suggests to the master carpenter as surely as it does
> to the sublime Euler . . . from experience and from
> study . . . and I demand next sensibility.[37]

Diderot asserts that taste and sensibility are separate notions. A man might have sensibility and simply admire an object without being able to give any reasons for his admiration. Another man might have a great deal of sensibility, or appreciation, but not be much moved by anything.

The most surprising corollary of the second antinomy, and the one that so sharply reveals Diderot's struggle between the

Ancien Régime and the rising wave of romanticism, is hinted at in his *Discours de la poésie dramatique.* The true dramatist must begin with a strong idea, a strong concept, and proceed to give the rules to *la belle nature.* In the introduction to the *Salon de 1767* Diderot asserts that the difference between the genius and the man of talent is that the latter faithfully imitates nature and presents nature as it really exists. The genius seeks the true model, which is a hybrid of his own imagination and the manifold of nature, and interprets his subject. It is not that genius allegorizes; Diderot's dislike of allegory is well known:

> Prefer, as much as it is possible, real personages to symbolic beings. . . .
>
> Allegory, rarely sublime, is almost always cold and obscure.[38]

Rather, the artist of genius attaches himself to the particular object, which is in some way at the same time the ideal model. One also notes a struggle between naturalism and idealism in Diderot's aesthetics.

It would be impossible to reconcile these various notions that Diderot presents, because many are in flagrant contradiction with others. One can only say that the neoclassical notion of imitation, as we examined it at the beginning of the present chapter, has been greatly altered and modified. It is no longer nature which gives laws to men, but men who gives laws to nature. One is reminded of Kant's Copernican revolution in philosophy; Diderot appears to have effected a similar revolution in aesthetics.

Although Diderot's article on "Beau" is his most carefully reasoned statement concerning the roles of imitation and creation, it should not be taken, however, as his definitive thought on the matter, and we should not use the text as a canonical touchstone to which all of his other writings should be referred.

We must bear in mind that the other treatments of creation which appear in *Paradoxe sur le comédien*, the *Salon de 1767*, and *De la poésie dramatique* were written some twenty years later. Unless a man is so benighted as to believe that he has hit upon the absolute truth, his thought inevitably grows and alters. If we desired an historical exegesis of Diderot's thought, we should have to trace his development year by year, giving special attention to the dates of his works, but for a philosophical analysis of his thought such a procedure is not necessary. What is necessary, however, in order to appreciate his more mature views on creation, is to turn to his theories concerning imagination and genius. We shall find, I hope, that of all the theorists of the Enlightenment, Diderot gives the most detailed account of artistic creation.

Since imagination plays such an important part in Diderot's theory of creation, it would be best to formulate his conception of its function and limits. Although Diderot shared many of the ideas of the Enlightenment, he harbored certain of the mistrusts of the imagination that philosophers of the seventeenth century had also felt. Descartes, Leibniz, and Spinoza had been wary of the imagination because it belonged to the irrational side of man's nature. According to the continental rationalists, the imagination is one of the chief causes of error and folly because it is given to recompounding the images from reality without obeying the laws of nature or of logic. Thus a man carried away by emotion readily confuses the vagaries produced by his imagination with reality; the result is sometimes religious persecution, sometimes superstition, sometimes war, and almost always unhappiness. The only correct role of the imagination, according to the rationalists, was to supply a pictorial aid to the understanding similar to, for example, the models and diagrams one gives to students learning geometry. Even though Diderot was less severe in his condemnation of the imagination, he was far from elevating it to the romantic heights found in Baudelaire. Diderot also eschews imagination in his prose style; he uses few images and ornaments, and he expresses himself directly and simply. In his fictional writings one encounters few descriptions and no imaginative rhapsodies. All is clear, dry, and quick.

Diderot defines the imagination as the faculty of recalling images or the appearances of objects. It goes without saying that imagination presupposes memory. He wants to hold, however, that imagination recalls specifically the forms and colors of objects, whereas memory recalls ideas and meanings. Imagination is concrete, particular, and sensible; memory is abstract, general, and intellectual. In the *Lettre sur les aveugles*, Diderot holds that imagination is primarily visual; it presents pictures and streams of pictures. Although there is nothing in the imagination which was not first in reality, imagination can recombine, reform, and enlarge upon the images reproduced from nature. When Diderot speaks of the poet, he means not merely one who writes verses but anyone who refashions the data reproduced by the imagination.

In his article *Sur le génie* he denounces *l'esprit observateur* as a petty spying upon the words and actions of other persons; artistic imitation creates.[39] Just what Diderot means by "create" we shall try to determine in a few moments. It should be noticed at this point that the imagination of a man of talent and that of a man of genius is, according to Diderot, a matter of degree. The genius is not a special sort of animal that has a privileged mode of knowledge but is, rather, one whose "soul is broader, struck by the sensations of all beings, interested in everything that goes on in nature, and whose every idea awakens a sentiment."[40] The imagination of the genius recalls images with more feeling than it received them, because it links each image with numerous others. It is not the imagination that distinguishes the man of genius from the man of talent but, rather, a precision of perception:

> It exerts itself without effort, without contention; it does
> not look, it sees, it instructs itself, it broadens itself
> without studying, . . . it is a rare machine that says "That

117

will succeed"—and it succeeds. "That will not succeed"—
and it does not succeed. . . . This sort of prophetic
spirit is not the same in all conditions of life; each has
its own. It is not guaranteed against errors, but the
errors which it occasions never entail contempt. . . . The
man of genius knows that he is playing with chances,
and he knows it without calculating the chances for or
against.[41]

Two characteristics separate the imagination of talent from
that of genius—spontaneity and empathy. Talent is the result
of much study and the knowledge of a multitude of rules; its
products are conventionally beautiful. Genius is a gift of nature and "is transported into the situation of the personages
which it animates."[42]

The love of this eternal beauty which characterizes nature
and the passion to form his models after some indefinable model which he has created and according to which
he has the ideas and sentiments of beauty—these
constitute the taste of the man of genius.[43]

One must not, he warns us, confuse an interior model with
an exterior one. The interior is the object of the active or creative imagination, whereas the exterior is the result of mere
copying. The interior model is the result of empathy with the
objects or situations which the artist reproduces in a sensuous
medium. The model is rendered vibrant by enthusiasm, which
is a force that nullifies the temporal and physical boundries of
objects.

As we noticed earlier, Diderot denies that even the imagination of the genius creates in any real sense of the term, for the
imagination only recomposes and enlarges upon what is given
in nature. We must take Diderot to mean by "create," "create
out of nothing," and, consequently, it becomes a truism for him

to say that the artistic genius does not create. No matter how strange and rich the work of the genius might be, it is still the elements of reality that have suffered the change in his imagination. Nevertheless, Diderot distinguishes sharply between rearranging the elements of nature and artistic creation. In the *Salon de 1767* he asserts that a painting by Loutherbourg is "made and well made. The Vernet is created."[44] With his theories of the imagination in hand, let us try to formulate a more precise statement of Diderot's conception of artistic creativity.

It is to be noted first of all that artistic talent is very close to scientific. One could deduce this view from Diderot's distrust of the imagination and his great esteem of the fine arts. If the arts were chiefly imaginative productions, and if artistic talent were simply an overexuberance of the imagination, Diderot could not consistently accord the arts such a high place in the activities of man. As Diderot mentions in the *Paradoxe*: "Sensibility is hardly the quality of a great genius. He will love justice but will exercise this virtue without reaping any of its sweetness. It is not his heart but his head which does everything."[45]

Given that artistic genius is close to scientific, it would follow that artistic creation would take its roots from an exacting analysis of nature. Diderot writes in the *Éloge de Richardson*:

> You have seen the sunset and the rising of the stars a
> hundred times; you have heard the countryside break out
> in the song of birds; but who among you have felt that
> it was the noise of day which made the silence of the
> night more touching? It is the same thing for physical
> phenomena as for moral; bursts of passion have often
> struck your ears, but you are far from knowing all the
> secrets of their accents and expressions. . . . The art of
> the great poet is to show you a fugitive circumstance
> that had escaped you.[46]

Similarly, the art of fiction, so Diderot holds, is closer to science than to history, for history relates only the actions and comportment of individuals. The novelist is interested in describing the human species and the general contours of human behavior.[47] Again, the artist and the scientist resemble one another in that both can make errors in selecting from experience; they might, for example, seize upon something anomalous and take it for the norm. Diderot charges the painter Baudouin with having ill chosen his subject matter in the same way that one might charge a scientist for not giving the adequate or proper experimental evidence for a theory.[48] In writing about La Tour[49] Diderot draws still another comparison between the artist and the scientist; both must look at nature without prejudices and without the encumbrances of convention. The painter who sees nature through the veil of academic rules, or through the eyes of other painters, will produce either stiff set pieces or mere imitations. Although an artist approaches nature with an hypothesis—a subject or theme he wants to show—he ought not to impose alien rules upon the data of experience.

Despite the many similarities between the artist and the scientist, Diderot recognizes that there are marked differences between the two. The artist not only can but ought to give a multitude of interpretations to the same objects in nature. Artists are not so much interested in establishing the truth as in the plausibility of a certain way of looking at the world. Nature is presumed to be uniform for the scientist, and, consequently, all adequately trained scientists should come to the same conclusions. In the *Salon de 1767* Diderot describes the difference with precision:

> But nature being one, how is it that there are so many
> diverse ways of imitating it, and that one approves of all
> of them? Does it not arise from the fact that, given the
> recognized and perhaps happy impossibility of rendering
> nature with an absolute precision, there is a mid-ground
> of convention upon which art is allowed to walk. Does

it not also arise from the fact that in all poetic production
there is always a bit of falsehood, the limits of which
are not and will never be determined? . . . Once one has
admitted that the sun of the painter is not and could not
be that of the universe, is one not committed to another
confession from which an infinity of consequences follow?
The first of which is not to demand of art to go beyond
its resources; the second is to pronounce with an extreme
circumspection upon all scenes in which everything is
in agreement.[50]

One of the most important conclusions to draw from
Diderot's comparison of the artist with the scientist is that artistic creativity is not a species of self-expression. The theory
of art as expression was to gain a stronghold in Europe during
the nineteenth century, but there are few traces of this theory
to be found in Diderot. Rather, the artist is one who creates a
new model or image which is capable of transmitting a fresh
conception of some aspect of nature or of the interior life of
man. The poet multiplies upon the basis of the given by the
process of analogy; the imagination is carried by insensible
gradations beyond nature. The result is that in a work of art
one has the feeling of familiarity coupled with the awareness
that everything has been slightly altered. What Diderot says
in the *Paradoxe* of sculpture, he holds to be true of all the fine
arts. Artists copy the first model that presents itself and then
see that there are less imperfect models which are preferable.
Sculpture corrects the gross defects of the second set of models,
then the minor defects, and "by a long suite of work, sculpture
attains a figure which is no longer part of nature."[51] Diderot's
final view of artistic creation is that it is a process of increasing
rarification of natural data by means of analogies; the result is
the formation of a new model or view of the world presented
in a sensuous medium. We have come a long way from the
simplistic theories of the imitation of *la belle nature* which we
encountered at the beginning of the Enlightenment.

IV Art, Language, and Morality

BECAUSE the aestheticians of the Enlightenment had many theories concerning the social and moral importance of the fine arts, it will be convenient and, I hope, illuminating to use the term "morality" in a broad sense. In general, the writers of the period were interested in showing, and sometimes in criticizing, the role of the arts in the social institutions of mankind. Certain writers attempted to reveal the influence of the arts upon the mores or customs of society. Other writers engaged in homily and in sermonizing; they tried to dictate to the artist what kind of human being he should be in order to be worthy of the epithet "artist." Still other writers advanced theories concerning the origin of the arts in primitive society; we shall encounter a number of interesting genetic explanations of artistic activity. And finally certain philosophers tried to show that the aesthetic life of man is indissolubly wedded with his moral life.

The spur to philosophical speculation has often been a concern to discover what kind of life a man ought to lead. Socrates, for example, confesses in several of Plato's dialogues that it was the quest for the nature of ethical goodness which led him into the intricacies of metaphysical speculation. Kant states that he made his way through his epistemological labyrinth in order to show how man is a free moral agent in a deterministic universe. One need only cite the title of Spinoza's major work, *Ethics Demonstrated in the Geometric Manner*, to show that even philosophers who were profoundly interested in mathematics were driven on by preeminently moral concerns. We shall find a similar concern among the aestheticians of the French Enlightenment. One might be surprised that morality preoccupied thinkers in a period often described as debauched and frivolous. But as the Goncourt brothers observe in the preface to their *La Femme au dix-huitième siècle*,[1] historians have feared to be noted for *légèreté* in writing about a century in which lightness was only the surface and the mask. In this chapter we shall notice that entertainment and mere diversion were held to be far removed from the purpose of the fine arts.

It is not, however, to the *Encyclopédie* that we should turn for a detailed examination of the role of the fine arts. Although the *Encyclopédie* was the first illustrated compendium of the arts and crafts to appear in Europe, its tone was uneven, it was riddled with errors, and it embarked from many philosophical ports—materialism, deism, sensualism, and that most meretricious port of all, eclecticism. The various entries on the fine and applied arts reveal that the *philosophes* have only a few bare generalities to offer: the arts ought to serve a useful purpose, the chief end of art is the moral improvement of mankind, and works of art fulfill their role by showing the ugliness of vice and the beauty of virtue. Nature is said to have an edifying and moral function, but, curiously, only a man of refined taste and of a moral bent can profit from nature. Technique is important because it enables the artist to instruct mankind. Other than these platitudinous assertions, the *Encyclopédie* affords little understanding of the social and moral roles of the fine arts. Diderot himself was aware of the deficiencies of the *Encyclopédie* and mentions that the articles on chemistry were "detestable," those on medicine "poor," those on literature "weak," and those on the fine arts "to be redone."

It is rather to Diderot that we must turn for one of the

major statements concerning the relationship between art and morality. As is to be expected, Diderot's thought on this subject is more perceptive than coherent and more spontaneous than analytic, but, as is also to be expected, what he has to say is of great importance and interest. The problem of dating presented in the previous chapter concerning imitation and creation does not arise here, for Diderot barely changed his opinions on morality during the course of his various writings. Although his views become more detailed and exact, his principles remain the same. Before tracing Diderot's thought concerning the relationships between art and morality, it will be best to make clear the salient features of his ethics, otherwise his theory of aesthetic happiness will make little sense.

Like most thinkers of the Enlightenment Diderot assumed that there exists a universal human nature which has not altered and will never alter throughout the course of history. Human nature among the ancient Greeks is the same as that encountered among eighteenth-century Parisians. It is true that aberrant personalities exist and that strange departures from the norm occur, but Diderot assumes, and rightly, that a few defective or anomalous specimens of a species do not constitute a sufficient reason for denying the existence of the species itself. That a class of objects shares a number of common and peculiar properties gives us warrant to speak of the nature of the objects or of their essence. To examine whether Diderot is right in assuming that human nature is constant would carry us far afield. I personally believe that he is mistaken. What is of importance, however, is to examine the way in which he describes the ethical aspect of human nature.

Following the philosophy of Locke, with which he was well acquainted, Diderot denies the existence of innate ideas. Man is not born with certain propositions, such as the existence of God or the criteria of truth and falsehood, imprinted upon his mind. Diderot asserts that certain persons have been led to believe in the existence of innate ideas because habits are so quickly and imperceptibly acquired that they seem to be part of man's nature. Upon scrutiny, however, we shall always discover that certain customs and institutions of society are the causes of what appear to be innate ideas.

According to Diderot, human nature is causally determined; for every change and mutation in man's thought and behavior there exists a necessitating cause. But as we shall shortly see, Diderot has an elaborate and sophisticated theory of human freedom and happiness, which is the first aesthetic theory of human freedom to appear in Western philosophy.

Human nature is not only determined, it is also materialistic. Diderot does not accept the long tradition of the dichotomy between the body and the soul. Passages abound in his writing to prove this point, but I shall choose only two, both drawn from his writings on aesthetics. In the *Paradoxe sur le comédien* we find an interchange between *le Premier*, who is in all likelihood Diderot himself, and *le Second*, who is of the same opinion as Diderot concerning materialism. After *le Premier* asserts that "the great dramatic poets above all are assiduous spectators of everything which goes on around them both in the physical world and the moral,"[2] *le Second* replies, "Which are one and the same thing."[3] Because of its brilliance, the second passage deserves to be quoted at length. After asking how it is that the poet, the orator, the painter, and the sculptor can be so unequal in their respective productions, Diderot asserts:

It is an affair of the moment, a state of the body, a state of the soul, a little domestic quarrel, a caress given to his wife in the morning before going to his workshop, two droplets of lost fluid which contained all the fire and the heat and the genius, a child who said or did something stupid, a friend who lacked delicacy, a mistress who received too familiarly someone indifferent. How can I put it? A bed too cold or too hot, a blanket that slipped off during the night, a pillow badly placed, half a glass of wine too much, a gastric disorder, one's hair ruffled under a night bonnet—and farewell to one's verve. There is something of chance in chess and in all the other games of the mind. And why should there not be? Where was the sublime idea the moment before it presented itself? What does it depend upon to come or not to come? What I know is that it is so tied to the fatal order of the poet's and the artist's life that it could not have come sooner or later, and it is absurd to suppose that it is the same thing in another being, in another life, or in another order of things.[4]

Two words in this passage, "soul" and "chance," might have struck the reader as incongruous with what I have said about Diderot's materialistic determinism. But it is important to notice that Diderot often uses the language of the multitude even though he continues to think as a philosopher. When Diderot speaks of "chance," he does not mean some event for which there is no cause but rather an event which is either unexpected or undesirable. A chance event, for Diderot, is one that is intimately linked in the fatal order of the life of the poet, for example, but which causes the poet to write badly. Moreover, when Diderot writes that "it is an affair of the moment, a state of the body, a state of the soul," it is important to observe that he does not link the last two phrases by "and." It is as if Diderot said, with a vague gesture of the hand, the body and the soul are the same thing. Although it is undeniable that Diderot is inconsistent with himself on a number of subjects, many scholars have exaggerated his inconsistencies by failing to notice that he uses the words of everyday language with a new turn.

To use the vocabulary of the philosophical trade, it would be for the most part accurate to characterize Diderot as a teleological utilitarian. If one ignores minor inconsistencies and a few scattered passages, the dominant impression one receives from Diderot's writings on ethics is that all human action tends toward a goal, and that the goodness of an action is in proportion to its utility. Conversely, the badness of an action is in proportion to its futility or nonusefulness. Diderot's account of the supreme goal of aesthetic freedom and happiness is, as I have already mentioned, something new in Western philosophy. But once again I shall defer discussion of his theory of aesthetic happiness until all the principles of his ethics have been enumerated.

Like many of his predecessors, Diderot was haunted by the belief that two warring powers lay siege to human nature. There is the force of egoism, which he does not equate with selfishness, and the force of altruism, which he does not equate with virtue. But unlike certain of his contemporaries, such as Bishop Butler, Diderot does not give a careful analysis of the respective powers of the two forces. Although Diderot tends to define virtue as a personal sacrifice for the general good and vice as a shortsighted insistence upon one's own momentary pleasures, he nevertheless tries to argue that virtue is not always to one's ultimate interest. At other points in his argument he appears to hold that virtue is nothing more than enlightened self-interest, and that the language of "having pity for," "sacrificing oneself for," and "generosity" is but a polite and urbane way of hiding the means to one's own interests. Even so, one encounters passages which flatly contradict the reduction of altruism to self-interest: "What is virtue? It is, according to whatever face one considers it, a sacrifice of oneself. The sacrifice that one makes of oneself in ideas is a preconceived disposition to immolate oneself in reality."[5]

When we are faced with such a contradiction in as serious a philosopher as Diderot, when we try to determine whether he is really an ethical altruist or an ethical egoist, a number of steps are at our disposal. The easiest, of course, is simply to pass on and say that the texts are contradictory, and that from a contradiction everything follows. But the only virtue of such a step is its facility. Again, we might count the number of passages in which he reduces the altruistic inclinations in man to the egoistic as opposed to the passages in which he writes that certain men both can and do wittingly sacrifice their own interest to that of other persons. But this method would have no logical consequence, since it would only reveal the number of times that he contradicted himself. Or again, we might refer to the author's life, for it is well known that Diderot was an extremely generous man, and that he often supported personal discomfort even though he knew it was not to his own interest. But the inconvenience of this method is its lack of logical cohesion; an author's life neither confirms nor disconfirms his philosophical principles. Lord Bacon might very well have accepted bribes, but the truth or falsity of his philosophy is another matter. What serves best to resolve the contradiction, I find, is the general tone of Diderot's fictional writings, especially *La Religieuse*, *Le Neveu de rameau*, and *Jacques le fataliste*. There one finds characters who are actuated by altruistic motives—personages who wittingly sacrifice their own good for the good of other persons, even though they are well aware that their actions will never augment their own happiness or even attenuate their misery. It appears that for Diderot virtue does not necessarily entail happiness, even though vice necessarily entails unhappiness.

I do not mean to argue that there is a logical relationship between the propositions of Diderot's fiction and the propositions of his philosophy. The former kinds of sentences are in an important sense neither true nor false, while the latter are purportedly either true or false. What I suggest is that Diderot's fiction is a strong persuasive argument for believing that his ethical philosophy is very much like that of the ordinary man: human beings act for the most part out of self-interest but are capable of acting disinterestedly and are sometimes morally obliged to do so.

Diderot's belief that moral goodness is dictated by man's nature and not by God or some other superhuman power clearly makes him a naturalist. Ethical goodness consists in successful adaptation to man's nature and in purposeful development; evil consists in the contrary. Ideally, a moral code would be a set of rules that reveal the best ways for mankind to achieve his organic needs. Mankind without nature is powerless; nature without man is amoral. It is the introduction of man into the world that engenders the distinction between good and evil.

The final tenet of Diderot's ethics that needs mentioning before turning to his aesthetics is the belief, hardly uncommon in the eighteenth century, in the inherent rationality of man. Human beings are supposed to be eminently amenable to rational persuasion. Moral education is not a mere pandering to man's natural desires but an attempt to show him what is to his real interest. Once a man knows what he ought to do he cannot but act accordingly.

With the structure of Diderot's ethics in mind, we are now in the position to appreciate his views concerning the moral function of art. As for artists themselves, he maintains that they must be profoundly moral persons in order to create:

> If you are well born, if nature has given you a sense of rectitude and a sensible heart, flee for a while the commerce of men; go study by yourselves. How can an instrument produce correct harmony if it is not in tune? . . . If you have vice to describe, know how greatly it is contrary to the general good and to private and public happiness. . . . If it is virtue, how will you be able to speak of it in a way to make others love it if you are not yourselves transported?[6]

Not only must artists be morally superior persons—a notion which recalls Milton's advice that a poet must himself be a great poem in order to write about things worthy to be re-membered by posterity—but all the productions of the artist must have a moral aim. In the *Éloge de Richardson*, Diderot founds the major part of his praise of Richardson on the moral purport of his fiction. After asserting that most persons un-derstand by the word *novel* "a tissue of frivolous and chimeri-cal events the reading of which is dangerous to state and mor-als,"[7] Diderot describes Richardson as one who "raises the mind, touches the soul," and whose works "breathe the air of goodness."[8] In the works of Richardson one mixes oneself with the conversation, approves, blames, admires and becomes morally indignant. "My soul was in a state of continual agita-tion. How good I was! How just I was! . . . I was, after fin-ishing reading, what a man is at the end of a day that he has spent doing good."[9] What Diderot says of fiction, he appears to hold in regard to all the verbal arts.

His insistence on the moral content of art often leads his judgement astray. After announcing to artists: "If you are concerned about the longevity of your works, I counsel you to occupy yourselves with honest subjects. Everything that teaches depravation to man is made for destruction,"[10] he is led to condemn Boucher because:

> Painting has this in common with poetry . . . that both must be morally good; both must have morals. Boucher does not suspect it; he is always vicious. . . . I would dare to say to Boucher: "If you address yourself only to a scamp of eighteen years, you are right, my friend. Continue to paint buttocks and breasts."[11]

It was not that Diderot was insensitive to the purely for-mal aspects of painting, for in his criticism of Chardin he notes the distribution of masses and the careless but carefully planned composition.[12] Nonetheless, Diderot is much more interested in the content or subject of a painting than in its formal or technical properties. It might be that his overriding moral interests lead him into such errors as the one that occurs in his discussion of Vernet: "But if each isolated portion affects you in this way, what must be the effect of the ensemble!"[13] Surely, however, the aesthetic merit of a painting cannot be determined by adding up the merits of the particular parts. The same heavy emphasis upon morality explains his insensitivity to Watteau: "I make fun of him, and I shall persist."[14]

For all his liberality on political matters, Diderot is often unreasonably dogmatic in his aesthetics. Dogmatism is born of purblindness, and it is obvious that Diderot could not see what Poussin was attempting to do in his *Jupiter et Callistro*. Diderot legislates that "painting has only one instant; it is not allowed to embrace two instants any more than two actions."[15] But precisely what Poussin was attempting to do in *Jupiter et Callistro* was to show the progress of action and the effects of time in one and the same painting. Poussin was dealing with the same problems of temporality in painting that were to be more successfully handled by certain painters of the twentieth century.

Suffice it to say that Diderot's strong moral bent often renders his criticism priggish and insensitive. If it were not that he had an original and brilliant theory concerning the nature of aesthetic happiness and of aesthetic education, his criticism would have only an historical and documentary value. Let us first examine his theory of aesthetic happiness, and then his theory of the educative role of the fine arts.

As we have noticed, Diderot is a teleologist; it is also clear that he is a hedonist, but a hedonist of a very special sort, which I shall call "aesthetic." The factors that work against man's happiness are numerous: his selfish and arrogant nature, the laws and institutions of society, and religion. Diderot mentions that even capitalistic society and private property impede man's happiness. Instead of a social revolution to extirpate these impediments, Diderot proposes an aesthetic revolution.

It is the aesthetic imagination of the artist and aesthetic experience that deliver man from bondage. Although a human being is never free in the sense that his actions are uncaused or that he could have done otherwise, he experiences, according to Diderot, a sentiment of freedom which is caused by great art. The sentiment consists in a free play of the imagination controlled by a sensuous image. One has the impression of doing and of feeling exactly what one wants, and so one applies the word "free" to one's experience. In front of a Vernet, Diderot has the impression that he is existing like God; he has the feeling of timelessness, of serenity, and of ecstasy. It is as if he were no longer a particular individual with his private cares and grief but were confused with the eternal race of mankind. By creating a particular kind of model and analogy—a subject which I dealt with in the previous chapter in my discussion of Diderot—the artist enables man to enter into a better world.

Given the fragility of human bonds and the general sordidness of the world, a man cannot do better than turn to the fine arts for happiness. Religion offers only superstitions and political life only disappointments. Diderot describes the aesthetic experience as a break with the world, as a kind of suspended activity and serenity of the mind, as a detachment from the future, and as a feeling of good conscience. He holds that art is a greater and purer source of happiness than nature. Although he does not maintain that the experience of art is the only source of true happiness—for he is hardly insensitive to the voluptuous feelings of love and the pleasures of friendship —he holds that the experience of the fine arts offers an unparalleled feeling of repose and completeness. In describing the effects that Richardson has upon him, Diderot says: "He left me in a melancholy that pleases me and which endures. . . . Torn away from reading by serious occupation, I felt an unconquerable distaste."[16]

One also encounters a strong strain of romanticism in Diderot's description of aesthetic experience. Although he remains for the most part a classicist, as I tried to show in my discussion of Diderot's theory of the imagination, he is one of the first writers in eighteenth-century France to succumb to the wistful vagaries of artistic feelings. In describing his reaction to a painting by Hubert Robert, he says:

> The ideas which ruins awaken in me are great. Everything is destroyed, everything perishes, everything passes on. There is only the world which remains. There is only time which endures. . . . I walk between two eternities. From whatever point I cast my eye the objects which surround me announce an end and resign me to the one that awaits me. What is my ephemeral being in comparison with this crag that is crumbling, with this valley that is growing deeper, with this forest that is wavering. . . . I do not want to die![17]

In addition to the moral enlightenment provided by the fine arts, Diderot argues that the artist teaches the individual how to observe more accurately, how to be a more careful judge of human nature, and, above all, how to conceive of objects in a new way. It is as if particular works of art were elaborate analogies which the artist gives to persons, saying: "Try to see how this scene, this human situation, this familiar natural object can be conceived of in a new light." The second role of the arts is to develop the imaginative powers of man, which, as we noticed in the previous chapter in the discussion of Diderot, are closely akin to the intellectual powers. Art, therefore, helps the advance of the physical sciences. "When the taste of the fine arts is general among a nation, do you know what happens? It is that the eye of the people conforms to the eye of the great artist."[18]

Just as an actor can give a number of interpretations to the same lines of a play—"Conceive how easy and frequent it is for two interlocutors in employing the same expressions to have thought and said entirely different things"[19]—so, too, does the artist, such as Chardin, present familiar objects in such a way that the spectator has the impression of never having seen them before. Art is essentially a humanized interpretation of the universe.

The most marked departure from Diderot's earlier theory concerning relationships, which was presented in "Le Beau,"[20] appears in the *Pensées Détachées sur la peinture*[21] and in the *Salon de 1767*. In the early work the poet and the artist in general are said to discover or perceive relationships which are inherent in nature. Metaphors are discovered by the poet as if they were objectively given. In his later work Diderot gives a more accurate account of artistic activity. The artist invents or creates new relationships between objects, taking "objects" in the broadest sense to include visual objects, human situations, sounds, forms, and lines. Metaphors are proposals by the poet to the reader to consider a certain subject in a new way. For example, the poet might ask the reader to conceive of Delilah surrounded by her handmaidens in terms of a stately galleon floating and buoyed by lesser ships, or to conceive of a love affair in terms of a game of chess, or to imagine the actions of the mind in its imaginative activity as a nest of coals fanned by breezes. Although a metaphor can be fit or inapposite, original or hackneyed, it cannot be true or false. The great educative value of art is to broaden one's power to see the apposite- ness of imaginative constructions.

Although it is tempting to linger over the richness of Did- erot's writings on aesthetic happiness, the other writers of the period must not be neglected. Many other theories of the moral influence of the fine arts were advanced, and certain of them are of an entirely different bent from that of Diderot's. It is always a temptation to simplify the philosophical thought of an era and to attempt to establish a "spirit of the age." As we have seen throughout the course of the aesthetic thought of the French Enlightenment, there was no consensus on the major problems of aesthetics, and, therefore, it would be both impertinent and brutal to reduce the thought of the period to a general thesis. Let us now turn to other philosophers, some who held theories sharply opposed to those of Diderot, some who held views compatible with his own but which had a different emphasis, and some who were neither in accord nor in disaccord with Diderot but who were developing themes of their own.

One of the most interesting themes of the period is the one developed by Condillac. In his *Essai sur l'origine des connaissances humaines* he announces that he is going to reduce all human activities, including the fine arts, to a single principle. As we have noticed, Condillac was not the first figure of the period to attempt such a feat; the passion for this type of reduction was widespread. By "reduce" Condillac obviously means "find the origin of," for he launches into the past history of man and tries to consider him in his primitive state. Again, Condillac's way of arguing was typical of the Enlightenment. To explain the nature of something, or to show how some state of affairs is reached, the philosopher of the Enlightenment often gives a genetic explanation. One encounters the same way of arguing in treatises on the philosophy of law, on epistemology, and on ethics. To explain the role of the fine arts and their social importance, then, Condillac tries to explain how they arose in the history of man.

The reader might like to interrupt Condillac even before the "single principle" is presented, for knowing the history or genesis of something does not entail an explanation of why something is what it is. For example, the practice of handshaking might have arisen, so certain anthropologists tell us, out of the desire to be sure that the other fellow was not armed. It would not follow, however, that Western people continue to shake hands in order to know that the other fellow is not hiding a knife or a hatchet. Although genetic explanations have their place, it is not in philosophy.

Let us waive these scruples, however, and see how Condillac tries to explain the role of the fine arts. The first principle of all human activities, he argues, is the language of action. It is a mute, nonverbal way of communicating certain desires and attitudes to other persons. Although the language has no verbal signs, it has physical signs—grimaces, facial expressions, gestures, and poses of the body. The language also has a syntax or a set of conventional rules concerning the order and sequence of the nonverbal signs. The language of action served man well during his infancy, but as his desires grew, his need to explain himself became more pressing. He had to find a more exact way of communication. Man first used the token, or the verbal sign, in order to abbreviate and render more precise his dealings with other persons. Signs were arbitrarily chosen; there was no resemblance between the noise of words and the objects or events for which they were the signs. Condillac asserts that the moment man began using verbal signs memory appeared:

> But as soon as a man begins to attach ideas to the signs
> he has chosen, one sees memory form in him. Once this
> is acquired, he begins to make use of his imagination
> and give it a new exercise. For, by the help of signs, he
> can recall at his will. He awakens, or at least can often
> awaken, the ideas to which they were attached.[22]

We must take Condillac to mean that the power of memory becomes more developed with the use of signs and not that memory suddenly appears when he begins to use a verbal language, for man would have had to have memory to use the language of action as well. It is also to be noted that Condillac's theory of language is rather primitive. He assumes that words are labels for ideas, and that ideas somehow float about in the mind waiting for names, like unborn infants. But though much could be said about Condillac's theory of language, I shall skirt these problems because they do not bear directly upon the topic with which we are dealing.

The first language, or the language of action, was "from its beginning proportioned to little intelligence . . . and consisted only in violent contortions and agitations."[23] Even when man began using articulate language he often used sign language and the language of action as well.

After the language of gestures came the first of the fine arts, the dance, which was used to express inward feelings, especially joy. The more complicated feelings are, the more complicated the dance becomes. As desires and feelings became more intricate, the dance was combined with articulate language to form drama on the one hand and music on the other. Just as articulate language grew richer and finally developed into poetry, so the language of gesture developed into highly abstract dancing.

Condillac adds, however, that poetry is only a primitive state of language. One can judge the sophistication of a race or a culture by its recourse to poetry. If the culture habitually expresses itself in poetic terms, in metaphors, and in imagery, then the culture is still in its infancy. If it avoids metaphorical language and strives after unadorned clarity of expression, then the culture is moving forward. Metaphors, then, according to Condillac, are all ideally translatable into nonmetaphorical language without any loss of meaning. The origin of the metaphor was not in its ornamental or aesthetic value but was rather a desperate attempt to explain something for which one did not yet have adequate words: "Poetry and music were cultivated only to make known the religion, the laws, and to keep the remembrance of great men and what they have done for their society."[24]

Painting, so Condillac argues, also developed because of man's overwhelming need to express himself. At the beginning painting was nothing more than writing, that is, setting down likenesses of objects or hieroglyphics. "It is quite probably the case that it is to the necessity of tracing our thoughts that painting owes its origin, and this necessity has doubtless helped to conserve the language of action which could most easily be painted."[25]

Man is primarily an active animal that has desires, not all of which can be immediately fulfilled. He must often wait and see what fortune has in store for him or attempt to rearrange matters. Consequently he turns not only to spoken language and mime but also to the various fine arts. Sometimes real desires are in part satisfied by illusory or artistic objects. Condillac is nonetheless aware that

> perhaps one will take all of this for a novel; but one cannot at least refuse it a certain verisimilitude. . . . I have seen in the language of action the germ of the languages and of all the arts which could serve to explain our thoughts; I have observed the circumstances which have been proper to develop this germ; and not only have I seen the arts born but also I have followed their progress and explained their different characters. In a word, I have, so it seems to me, demonstrated clearly that the things which seem the most singular were the most natural in their time and what could only have happened.[26]

Although Condillac makes a strong case for the importance of the fine arts during the infancy of mankind, he is led by the logic of his principles to deny the importance of the arts once man has achieved maturity. Just as metaphors are crude and makeshift ways of expressing something for which there is a lacuna in the language, so too, argues Condillac, the arts are but temporary ways of expressing what will ultimately be expressed clearly. The arts progress technically and undergo various changes during their hybridization with religion and the state, but as a kind of human activity the arts will finally become superannuated.

Condillac's theory might explain why the arts used to be important, but it fails to explain why they continue to be important when other means of communication, for example, mathmatics and symbolic logic, have been greatly perfected. What appears to have led Condillac astray is his belief that the fine arts are a kind of language. There is unquestionably some ground for the comparison between the arts and language, for both are commonly said to communicate something. We speak of music as communicating certain moods and feelings, and of language as communicating a person's desires and intentions. But the comparison between the two cannot be carried too far without encountering important dissimilarities. Neither in painting nor in music is there anything to correspond to the verbal signs of language, though the rules of musical composition and certain kinds of classical painting do have a counterpart in the syntax of language. Moreover, it is obvious that a linguistic system of a certain people can become superannuated; it might be too cumbersome, too rigid, and finally be obliged to give way to another and more supple language. Egyptian hieroglyphics might have had their charm, but they left something to be desired in the way of subtlety and nuance. One wonders, however, what it would mean for the fine arts to become superannuated, or for a certain branch of the arts, for example, music, to become outmoded. It is clear that certain styles, forms, and themes might fall into desuetude, but it is not at all clear what it would mean to say that music as such might be replaced by a superior form of communication. It might be that someday people will lose interest in music altogether, and that musical instruments will only be found in glass cases in museums like fossils and the bones of prehistoric animals. But to lose interest in a branch of the fine arts, or in the arts in general, does not entail that they have given way to a superior form of communication. It would only entail that people have different interests or perhaps none at all. Condillac's theory of the inevitable superannuation of the fine arts is, therefore, ill taken and founded upon a faulty comparison.

Furthermore, if we were to accept Condillac's theory, we should have to accept his description of metaphor as applying to all of the fine arts. Condillac holds that just as a metaphor is ideally translatable into purely cognitive terms, so, too, a work of art should be ideally expressible in logical symbols. Though there are many metaphors which one can translate into literal terms without a loss of meaning, there are others, notably in Shakespeare and certain romantic poets, which seem untranslatable. It is not simply that concinnity would be sacrificed to a literal turgidness, but that part of the meaning, and not simply the emotional force, would be lost. Even if one did hold that all metaphors could be translated into literal language—no matter how lengthy or cumbersome it might be—one would not therefore have to hold that all works of art could be translated. The idea of translating a piano sonata or a painting—which Condillac would call "expressions"—into something else borders on meaningless. What would count as the translation of a piano sonata? The feelings of the artist who composed it? But then we should have, if anything, biography. In effect, Condillac, for all the ingenuity of his argument, has confused two separate notions: (1) X is a sign or symbol of Y; in this case the relationship is asymmetrical, and the sign in no way imitates that of which it is a sign; or (2) X expresses Y because X imitates Y; in this case the relationship is symmetrical, that is, X and Y have certain properties in common. One can translate a poem into another language, but one cannot express the same poem in another language.

Even though much more could be said about the theory of art as expression, we should be carried into the nineteenth century and into our own day. Condillac was the founder of a long tradition which was to include Croce, Gentile, Collingwood, and Santayana.

If Condillac was the founder of aesthetic expressionism, Dubos was the forerunner of theorists who conceive of art as a kind of game. Each of the fine arts has a set of conventional rules which, though they might vary from age to age and school to school, are held to be binding upon anyone who wishes to play that particular game. Art without rules is as meaningless as games without rules. Even though an artist might develop a new kind of art, he submits himself to a new set of principles concerning the arrangement of masses, or the use of colors, or the organization of time, or the manipulation of plot. The interpreter of a work of art is also playing a game for which precise rules can often be laid down. In playing a piano sonata, for example, there are a great number of rules concerning the ways in which the various "pieces," or notes, are to be used. The piano teacher might say, for instance, that the student broke a rule concerning timing; he put in or left out a beat. Or again, the student might have held a chord half a beat too long. The rules are always precise and can be stated without using the vague and impressionistic language of the art critic.

The fine arts, according to Dubos, act as a liberator from other activities that are equally governed by rules. While many nonaesthetic activities have sanctions attached to them, the rules of art can be broken or obeyed with impunity except that of discord or ugliness. The rule-governed arts present the passions without actually affecting human beings. It is as though one were witnessing an operation upon oneself, while everything but the mind is anesthetized. Dubos does not elaborate upon his theory of art as a game but quickly moves on, as though asking the reader to think about the comparison himself. Dubos concludes:

> When real and true emotions procure the soul the most lively sensations and have such annoying consequences (because the happy moments they make felt are followed by such sad days), could not art find a means to separate the bad consequences of the bulk of the passions from that which is agreeable? Could not art create, so to speak, beings of a new order? Could it not produce objects

142

which excite in us artificial emotions, capable of occupying us in the moment that we feel them, and incapable of causing in us the real and painful consequences of true afflictions?[27]

Given the existence of the fine arts, Dubos's questions become rhetorical.

According to Dubos man is essentially a maker and a follower of rules; even during his playful moments man wants the range of possibilities limited. The lack of rules disquiets him and makes him ill at ease. Moreover, human feelings are often unwieldy and unbeautiful. One of the chief social purposes of art, so Dubos argues and with considerable force, is to liberate man from human emotions but at the same time to restrict his imagination by means of a controlled field—a musical composition, a tragedy, or a painting. The artificial emotions, as Dubos calls them, involve our recognizing that a certain scene in a play, for example, is tragic, without our having to suffer ourselves. In Dubos's writings one finds traces of a theory that was to be greatly developed later by Schopenhauer: art delivers man from the bondage of the will and places him in a nirvana of lawful lawlessness.

Many of the philosophers whom we have been studying frequented the salons of the most important ladies of the Enlightenment. Fontenelle often visited the salon of Madame de Lambert, while d'Alembert, Marmontel, and Caylus frequented the salon of Madame Geoffrin. She was well installed in the rue Saint Honoré, where she also received Montesquieu, Marivaux, and other persons who wrote philosophical reflections on the fine arts. There was also the salon of Madame Necker, the antechamber of the Revolution, where Buffon often appeared. Given the decor of the salons and the general curiosity about the origins of things, it was only natural that conversation should turn to the role of the fine arts in society. And it was

143

even more natural, given so much time for leisure and amusements, that art should often be conceived of as an escape from boredom or ennui. Montesquieu writes in this regard:

> Thus everything fatigues us in the long run, and above all the great pleasures; one leaves them always with the same satisfaction that one took them on, for the fibers that constitute the organs which felt them are in need of rest. . . . Our soul is tired of feeling, but not to feel is to fall into an annihilation that overwhelms one. One remedies everything by varying the modifications, and one does not languish.[28]

Montesquieu appears to hold that the arts were invented in and for an aristocratic society. Doubtless the common people had their own ways of diverting themselves, but these ways would not do for persons who had enjoyed all the pleasures and experienced all the emotions that the world has to offer.

The fear of ennui might have led to the overly subtle feelings and manipulation of sentiments that one finds in Marivaux; it might also have led to the perverse productions of the Marquis de Sade. But it is evident that an author always writes for a particular public and sets himself before a particular kind of audience, even if he idealizes it. From this it follows that the quality of the writing is in proportion to the quality of the audience. One cannot help concluding, along with many writers of the Enlightenment, that an aristocracy—not of birth, but of intelligence and sensibility—is essential for an age to produce great art.

According to Crousaz, three principal qualities empower objects to deliver us from ennui: grandeur, novelty, and diversity. Nature unaided by man is too uniform and predictable to entertain us for long. Batteux is in accord with Crousaz—we yearn for a new order of things which nature cannot give us. The fine arts rearrange the elements of nature in order to give our sentiments a new turn and our ideas a new perspective. The susceptibility to boredom, then, is one of the most useful attributes of man; without it we would slip into a porcine serenity, and the fine arts would degenerate into monotony.

Certain figures of the French Enlightenment who held that art must have a moral function merely repeated a theme that had been sounded for centuries in Western civilization, without composing any variations on it. As is well known, Rousseau believed that the fine arts were pernicious because they corrupt one's natural goodness. Beauty must be natural and unadorned, and, therefore, nature is the source not only of artistic but also of moral value. Rousseau was one of the first writers of the period to hold that the beauties of nature are superior to those of the arts. One wonders, however, if the attempt to rate the respective merits of each is not a puerile exercise, for the two are greatly different. One never speaks of the technical prowess of nature, one never asks what the artistic aim or purpose of a natural object is, one never engages in criticism of nature in the sense that one does of the fine arts. It is well and good if a man likes the great outdoors, as Rousseau did, and even better if a man derives some therapeutic or moral benefit from it. But it is not at all clear what it means to set one over the other, as Rousseau does, and insist upon the moral preeminence of nature.

The old theme that art gives moral lessons in sensuous media, providing both instruction and pleasure, also reappears among certain writers. Taillasson, for example, writes:

> Painting seems to be divisible into two principal parts, one decoration, the other expression; the end of the one is to please the eye, the end of the other to instruct and to charm both the mind and the heart. The success of the former is obtained by a happy design in regard to general proportions, . . . the effect of the second depends above all upon truth.[29]

Certain writers observe that aesthetic beauty is only a concession made to the frailness of man. If man were purely intellectual, he would not need the sensuous presentation of morality that the fine arts give him. Father André, for example, writes:

> If we had only pure intelligence for auditors or at least
> more reasonable men, in order to satisfy them we would
> only have to expose to them the simple truth. It would
> be sufficient to charm them, by its own light, by the order
> of principles which demonstrate truth. . . . It is beauty
> alone that one demands from a work of mathematics. . . .
> Therefore it is necessary in a discourse to present not
> only truth to satisfy the mind but also to clothe the truth
> with images in order to interest the imagination.[30]

This way of putting the matter, however, better describes the role of nursery tales and the illustrations one gives to children than the role of the fine arts. If one pushed André's theory to its logical conclusion, one would be committed to a theory like that of Condillac: art contains the seeds of its own superannuation.

Toward the end of the Enlightenment, certain writers interpreted the moral role of art in a highly chauvinistic manner. In the year VI (i.e., 1798) a text appeared by a certain Publicola Chaussard which was entitled *Essai Philosophique sur la dignité des arts*. This is the only philosophical text with which I am acquainted that is written almost entirely in the imperative mood. During the course of his admonitions to artists, Chaussard writes:

> Consult, imitate the simplicity of the antique severity. . . .
>   Artists, you are French; treat only national subjects.
> Associate your success with those of your country. . . .
>   Attach yourselves to the ideal beauty, to the faithful

imitation of nature, to expression. The miracles of Greek art arose from these principles.[31]

However useful the sentiment of nationalism might be for a political leader to rally the people of a fallen or divided country around him, whatever solace it might give to a people who are secretly aware of their country's defects, in the long run nationalism does not carry a nation very far, and it never advances humanity in general. The fine arts, like the sciences, are international; to require them to support the interests of a particular nation is to reduce the one to handicraft and the other to propaganda. Although there are some endeavors which do not require the talents of other nations to propagate themselves, like folklore, local customs, and popular art, the fine arts have always flourished during the periods of high commerce between great artistic powers. One has only to recall the Mycenaean influence upon the Athenians, or the rediscovery of antiquity during the Italian Renaissance, or the introduction of Italian modes under Francis I to realize that artists are as dependent upon the work of one another as are scientists. Artists working in seclusion, and producing works without knowing what is and has been going on around them, at best risk doing what has been done before and usually doing it badly. The result of artistic isolationism is the same as that of nationalistic isolationism: after a few flickerings of decadent mannerism, there follows a long darkness.

To trespass into the aesthetic literature beyond Chaussard's *Essai Philosophique*, however, or for that matter even into 1789, would involve breaking the limits I have set for myself in this study. Not only do the fine arts begin a process of marked decay in the early 1780s, but speculation on the fine arts becomes either eclectic and diffuse or chauvinistic propaganda. The literary salons which had given birth to so much speculation on the fine arts were soon to disappear. The enlightened amateur who had a penchant both for philosophy and

the arts would give way in the following century to the professional philosopher and the aesthetician. Not only were the
nobleness and elegance of the *Ancien Régime* to disappear entirely, but also the cosmopolitanism of thought, which was one
of the greatest merits of the French Enlightenment. Even so,
the four themes which we have discussed in this study would
reappear, long after the Enlightenment had come to a close, and
would form the basis of modern aesthetics.

Notes / Bibiography / Index

Notes

1. Baltimore, Md.: Johns Hopkins Press, 1959 and 1963 respectively.
2. London, 1902, 3 vols.
3. l'Abbé N. C. J. Trublet, *Essais sur divers sujets de littérature et de morale* (Amsterdam, 1755), pp. 5, 6.
4. All translations are my own.
5. Trublet, *Essais sur divers sujets*, p. 8.
6. "Do not strive to astonish the crowd; content yourself with few readers."
7. Trublet, *Essais sur divers sujets*, p. 217.

CHAPTER I: REASON AND SENTIMENT

1. Art. 85.
2. R. Descartes, *Traité des passions*, p. 180. All translations are my own.
3. J. P. Crousaz, *Traité du beau* (Amsterdam, 1715), p. 3.
4. Ibid., p. 3.
5. Ibid., p. 5.
6. Ibid., p. 4.
7. The writers with whom I am dealing tend to use the words *sentiment* and *coeur* interchangeably, just as they tend to use *esprit, entendement,* and *raison* with much the same signification. I have translated the French word *esprit* as *mind,* although the two words have connotations peculiar to each. Writers on the fine arts of the period were well aware of the ambiguity of the term *esprit.* Voltaire, for example, in his article "Esprit" in the *Encyclopédie,* asserts: "This word . . . is one of those vague terms to

151

which everyone who pronounces it almost always attaches a different sense. It expresses something other than judgement, genius, taste, talent, penetration, breadth of understanding, grace, fineness; and it must grasp all these merits. One could define it as 'ingenious reason'."

8. Crousaz, *Traité du beau*, p. 7.
9. Ibid.
10. Ibid.
11. Ibid., p. 2.
12. Ibid., p. 8.
13. Ibid., p. 9.
14. Ibid.
15. Ibid., p. 2.
16. Ibid.
17. Ibdi., p. 9.
18. Ibid.
19. Ibid., p. 67.
20. Ibid.
21. J. B. Dubos, *Réflexions Critiques sur la poésie, la peinture et la musique* (Paris, 1719), p. 474.
22. Ibid., p. 305.
23. Ibid., p. 306.
24. Ibid.
25. Ibid., p. 315.
26. Ibid., p. 316.
27. Ibid., p. 314.
28. It is perhaps worth mentioning that Voltaire, in the appendix to the *Siècle de Louis XIV* comments favorably on Dubos's *Réflexions Critiques sur la poésie*: "All the artists read with profit his 'Réflexions sur la poésie, la peinture et la musique'. It is the most useful book that has ever been written on these subjects in all the nations of Europe. What constitutes the merit of this book is that there are few errors and many true reflections, some new, some profound. It is not a systematic book, but the author thinks and makes the reader think."
29. Dubos, *Réflexions Critiques sur la poésie*, p. 328.
30. l'Abbé N. C. J. Trublet, *Essais sur divers sujets de littérature et de morale* (Amsterdam, 1755), p. 234.
31. Ibid., 2, p. 73.
32. Ibid., pp. 218, 219.
33. Ibid., p. 231.
34. Ibid., pp. 234, 235.
35. Pierre Estève, *L'Esprit des beaux-arts* (Paris, 1735), p. 4.
36. Ibid., p. 7.

37. Charles Bonnet, *Essai Analytique des facultés de l'âme* (Paris, 1717), pp. 3, 4, 5.

38. Charles Batteux, *Les Beaux-Arts réduits à un même principe* (Paris, 1746), p. 6.

39. Ibid., p. 7.

40. Ibid., p. 59.

41. Ibid.

42. Ibid.

43. Ibid.

44. Ibid.

45. Ibid., p. 63.

46. Ibid., p. 97.

47. Ibid., pp. 97, 98.

48. Ibid., p. 98.

49. le Père Yves André, *Essai sur le beau* (Paris, 1741), p. 1.

50. Ibid., p. 58.

51. Ibid., pp. 207, 208.

52. Crousaz, *Traité de beau*, p. 68.

53. Dubos, *Réflexions Critiques sur la poésie*, p. 6.

54. André, *Essai sur le beau*, p. 23.

55. Jean Baptiste d'Argens, *Réflexions Historiques et Critiques sur le goût* (Paris, 1743), pp. 1, 2.

56. *Encyclopédie*, p. 138.

57. Charles Rollin, *De la manière d'enseigner et d'étudier les belles-lettres* (Paris, 1726–1728), p. lxxxi.

58. Roger de Piles, *Diverses Conversations sur la peinture* (Paris, 1777), p. 37.

59. Rollin, *De la manière d'enseigner*, I, p. civ.

60. Alexandre Gérard, ed., *Essai sur le goût* (Paris, 1766), p. 236.

61. Ibid., p. 240.

62. Ibid., p. 241.

63. Jean d'Alembert, "Réflexions sur l'usage et sur l'abus de la philosophie dans les matières de goût," in *Essai sur le goût*, ed. Alexandre Gérard (Paris, 1766), p. 248.

64. Ibid.

65. Ibid., p. 249.

66. Ibid., pp. 261, 262.

67. Gérard, *Essai sur le goût*, p. 269.

68. Ibid.

69. Ibid.

70. Ibid., p. 270.

71. Ibid., p. 271.

72. Although Diderot's authorship of this work has often been contested, I have been convinced by the careful study in Lester G. Crocker's *Two Diderot Studies* (Baltimore, Md.: Johns Hopkins Press, 1952), pp. 115–17, that Diderot was the author. The *Recherchés Philosophiques sur l'origine et la nature de beau* appeared in the second volume of the *Encyclopédie*, which appeared in the bookshops during the last week of January 1752. But it should be noted that as recently as 1964, certain writers on aesthetics were not convinced that the *Recherchés* is by Diderot. George Boas, for example, in his "The Arts in the *Encyclopédie*," *The Journal of Aesthetics and Art Criticism*, 23, no. 1 (Fall 1964), pp. 97–107, asserts, "This article, since it is unsigned, should be by Diderot, but its emphasis on the cognitive aspects of the perception of beauty and particularly the phrase indicating that it is perceived in exactly the same way as the meanest notions would seem to indicate that d'Alembert was either its author or its inspiration" (p. 101).

73. Denis Diderot, *Recherchés Philosophiques*, translated from *Oeuvres Esthetiques*, ed. Paul Vernière (Paris, 1959), p. 417.

74. Ibid., p. 418.

75. Ibid., p. 426.

76. Ibid., p. 418.

77. Ibid.

78. Ibid., pp. 419, 420.

79. Ibid., p. 420.

80. Ibid., p. 419.

81. Ibid.

82. Ibid., p. 428.

CHAPTER II: RULES AND SPONTANEITY

1. Alexandre Gérard, ed., *Essai sur le goût* (Paris, 1766), p. 252. All translations are my own.

2. le Père Yves André, in his *Essai sur le beau* (Paris, 1741), p. 4, says wistfully, "You will realize how it is that if the *je-ne-sçai-quoi* did not come to their rescue, most aesthetic systems would not know how to reply to you."

3. J. P. Crousaz, *Traité du beau* (Amsterdam, 1715), p. 12.

4. Epistle 18.

5. A. de Marcenay de Ghuy, *Essai sur la beauté* (Paris, 1770), p. 6.

6. C. E. Briseux, *Traité du beau essentiel dans les arts* (Paris, 1752), p. 57.

7. I might be taken to task, I realize, for including Saint-Evremond in a work on the aesthetics of the eighteenth century, since he was born

around 1615 and died in 1703. Nevertheless, his works are often concerned with philosophical aesthetics instead of criticism, as I defined those terms in the Preface. For this reason I feel free to include him in the present work, but on the basis of the same distinction I believe that I am not obliged to include any of his contemporaries who did not write on aesthetics, for example, Boileau-Despréaux and Bouhours, however influential their criticism might have been in the eighteenth century.

8. C. de M. Saint-Evremond, *Oeuvres*, ed. Desmaizeaux (Paris, 1705), pp. 99–101.

9. Charles Batteux, *Les Beaux-Arts réduits à un même principe* (Paris, 1746), p. i.

10. Ibid., p. ii.

11. Ibid., p. 11.

12. Cf. Jean Ehrard, *L'Idée de nature en France dans le première moitié du XVIIIᵉ siècle* (Paris, 1963).

13. Batteux, *Les Beaux-Arts réduits*, p. 27.

14. Ibid., p. 42.

15. Ibid., p. 97.

16. Ibid., pp. 97–101.

17. Ibid.

18. Ibid.

19. Ibid.

20. Ibid., p. 100.

21. Ibid., p. 144.

22. Saint-Evremond, *Oeuvres*, 55, p. 100.

23. Saint-Evremond, "Sur les poèmes des anciens," *Oeuvres*, 4, p. 325.

24. Ibid.

25. Ibid., p. 335.

26. Ibid., p. 336.

27. Saint-Evremond, "De la tragédie ancienne et moderne," *Oeuvres*, 3, p. 171.

28. Briseux, *Traité du beau essentiel*, pp. 56–57.

29. Ibid., p. 60.

30. Anne Lefèbvre Dacier, *Des causes de la corruption du goût* (Paris, 1714), p. 3.

31. Ibid., p. 23.

32. Voltaire was hardly a consistent absolutist. One need only consult his famous definition of *beau* to see how closely he adhered to the relativist's position.

33. "Marion weeps, Marion cries, Marion wants someone to marry her." A. Houdard de la Motte, "Réflexions sur la critique: Réponse à Monsieur de Voltaire," p. 417.

34. J. G. Fontenelle, *Oeuvres Diverses*, 6 (Paris, 1740), p. 148.

35. Jean Joseph Taillasson, "Le Danger des règles dans les arts" (Paris, 1785), p. 3.

36. Jean Joseph Taillasson, *Observations sur quelques grands peintres* (Paris, 1807), pp. 11, 12, 13.

37. Jean Baptiste d'Argens, *Reflexions Historiques*, pp. 6, 7.

38. Roger de Piles, *Diverses Conversations sur la peinture* (Paris, 1777), p. 42.

39. Gérard, *Essai sur le goût*, p. 247.

40. Ibid., p. 274.

41. Ibid., p. 280.

42. Ibid.

43. I have not translated *basse latinité* so as not to rob it of any of its flavor.

44. Gérard, *Essai sur le goût*, p. 280.

45. C. L. de S. Montesquieu, *Espirit des lois* (Paris, 1784), pp. 189–90.

46. J. B. Dubos, *Réflexions Critiques sur la poésie, la peinture et la musique* (Paris, 1719), p. 2.

47. Ibid., pp. 4, 7.

48. Ibid., p. 21.

49. Ibid., p. 305.

50. Ibid., p. 313.

51. Ibid., p. 312.

52. Ibid.

53. Ibid., p. 310.

54. Ibid., p. 314.

55. Ibid., p. 309.

56. Ibid., p. 321.

57. Ibid., p. 399.

58. Ibid.

59. Ibid.

60. Ibid., pp. 316, 318.

61. Ibid., pp. 318, 321.

62. Ibid., p. 345.

63. Ibid., p. 376.

64. l'Abbé N. C. J. Trublet, *Essais sur divers sujets de littérature et de morale* (Amsterdam, 1755), pp. 138–40.

65. Batteux, *Les Beaux-Arts réduits*, pp. 138–40.

66. Crousaz, *Traité du beau*, p. 51.

67. Ibid., p. 72.

68. André, *Essai sur le beau*, p. 3.

69. Ibid., p. 8.

70. Ibid., p. 52.

71. de Marcenay de Ghuy, *Essai sur la beauté*, pp. 1–2.
72. Ibid., pp. 6, 9.
73. Ibid., p. 13.
74. Ibid., p. 18.
75. Ibid.
76. P. C. Marivaux, *Oeuvres Completes* (Paris, 1781), 9, p. 556.
77. Denis Diderot, *Pensées Détachées sur la peinture*, translated from *Oeuvres Esthetiques*, ed. Paul Vernière (Paris, 1959), p. 752.
78. Ibid., p. 753.
79. Ibid.
80. Ibid., pp. 758, 773.
81. Ibid., p. 758.
82. Denis Diderot, *L'Origine et la nature du beau*, translated from *Oeuvres Esthetiques*, ed. Paul Vernière (Paris, 1959), p. 435.
83. Ibid.
84. Ibid., p. 428.
85. I have drawn these eight criteria from Diderot's *Recherches Philosophiques sur l'origine et la nature du beau* (Paris, 1752) in which he speaks of the causes of diversity of taste. His twelve *sources* reduce to eight.

CHAPTER III: IMITATION AND CREATION

1. l'Abbé N. C. J. Trublet, *Essais sur divers sujets de littérature et de morale* (Amsterdam, 1755), pp. 221–22. All translations are my own.
2. Charles Batteux, *Les Beaux-Arts réduits à un même principe* (Paris, 1746), p. 25.
3. Ibid., p. 11.
4. Ibid., p. 31.
5. Ibid.
6. Ibid., p. 89.
7. Ibid., p. 96.
8. Denis Diderot, *Recherches Philosophiques sur l'origine et la nature du beau* (Paris, 1752), p. 22.
9. J. B. Dubos, *Réflexions Critiques sur la poésie, la peinture et la musique* (Paris, 1719), p. 52.
10. Ibid., pp. 225–26.
11. Ibid., p. 89.
12. Ibid.
13. Consult Voltaire's articles in the *Encyclopédie* entitled "Poète" and "Imagination," and Diderot's *Lettres sur les sourds et muets*.
14. A. Houdard de la Motte, *Oeuvres* (Paris, 1754), III, p. 190.

15. Jean Joseph Taillasson, *Observations sur quelques grands peintres* (Paris, 1807), p. 25.
16. Ibid., p. 93.

17. Il ordonna que toujours la nature
Seule fût du vrai beau. . . .

O vous de qui le coeur noblement agité
Brulez de s'élever a l'immortalité
Allez, volez vers elle, éclairé par la flamme
Que le maître des Dieux alluma dans votre âme:
Un tel guide jamais peut-il être trompeur?

Vous mettant à côté de vos rivaux fameux
Aillent servir de règle à vos lâches neveux (Jean Joseph Taillasson, "Le Danger des règles dans les arts" [Paris, 1785], pp. 5, 13, 14).
18. Roger de Piles, *Cours de peinture* (Paris, 1708), p. 2.
19. Ibid., p. 41.
20. Ibid., p. 44.
21. Dubos, *Réflexions Critiques sur la poésie*, I, pp. 1–2.
22. Ibid., pp. 28, 29–30.
23. Ibid., p. 25.
24. Ibid., pp. 29, 27.
25. Batteux, *Les Beaux-Arts réduits*, p. 94.
26. Ibid., p. 97.
27. J. P. Crousaz, *Traité du beau* (Amsterdam, 1715), p. 45.
28. Ibid., p. 20.
29. Denis Diderot, *Essais sur la peinture*, translated from *Oeuvres Esthetiques*, ed. Paul Vernière (Paris, 1959), p. 736.
30. Ibid., p. 738.
31. Ibid., p. 739.
32. Denis Diderot, *De la poésie dramatique*, translated from *Oeuvres Esthetiques*, ed. Paul Vernière (Paris, 1959), p. 379.
33. Denis Diderot, *Pensées Détachées sur la peinture*, translated from *Oeuvres Esthetiques*, ed Paul Vernière (Paris, 1959), p. 771.
34. Diderot, *Essais sur la peinture*, p. 741.
35. Diderot, *Recherches Philosophiques*, pp. 421, 422.
36. Ibid., pp. 418, 419.
37. Diderot, *Essais sur la peinture*, pp. 738, 739.
38. Diderot, *Pensées Détachées sur la peinture*, p. 766.
39. Denis Diderot, *Sur le génie*, translated from *Oeuvres Esthetiques*, ed. Paul Vernière (Paris, 1959), p. 19.

40. Ibid., p. 9.
41. Ibid., p. 20.
42. Ibid., p. 10.
43. Ibid., p. 12.
44. Denis Diderot, *Salon de 1767*, translated from *Oeuvres Esthetiques*, ed. Paul Vernière (Paris, 1959), p. 622.
45. Denis Diderot, *Paradoxe sur le comédien*, translated from *Oeuvres Esthetiques*, ed. Paul Vernière (Paris, 1959), p. 310.
46. Denis Diderot, *Éloge de Richardson*, translated from *Oeuvres Esthetiques*, ed, Paul Vernière (Paris, 1959), p. 35.
47. Ibid., pp. 39, 40.
48. Diderot, *Salon de 1767*, p. 470.
49. Ibid., p. 507.
50. Ibid., pp. 599, 600.
51. Diderot, *Paradoxe sur le comédien*, p. 399.

CHAPTER IV: ART, LANGUAGE, AND MORALITY

1. Paris: Librairie de Firmin-Didot, 1887.
2. Denis Diderot, *Paradoxe sur le comédien*, translated from *Oeuvres Esthetiques*, ed. Paul Vernière (Paris, 1959), pp. 309, 310. All translations are my own.
3. Ibid., p. 310.
4. Denis Diderot, *Salon de 1767*, translated from *Oeuvres Esthetiques*, ed. Paul Vernière (Paris, 1959), p. 579.
5. Denis Diderot, *Éloge de Richardson*, translated from *Oeuvres Esthetiques*, ed. Paul Vernière (Paris, 1959)), p. 37.
6. Denis Diderot, *De la poésie dramatique*, translated from *Oeuvres Esthetiques*, ed. Paul Vernière (Paris, 1959), p. 282.
7. Diderot, *Éloge de Richardson*, p. 29.
8. Ibid.
9. Ibid., p. 30.
10. Diderot, *Salon de 1767*, p. 471.
11. Denis Diderot, *Essais sur la peinture*, translated from *Oeuvres Esthetiques*, ed. Paul Vernière (Paris, 1959), p. 717.
12. Diderot, *Salon de 1767*, p. 493.
13. Ibid., p. 578.
14. Diderot, *Essais sur la peinture*, p. 714.
15. Ibid., p. 712.
16. Diderot, *Éloge de Richardson*, p. 33.
17. Diderot, *Salon de 1767*, p. 644.

18. Ibid., p. 507.

19. Diderot, *Paradoxe sur le comédien*, p. 304.

20. Circa 1752.

21. Circa 1765.

22. E. B. de Condillac, *Essai sur l'origine des connaissances humaines*, I (Amsterdam, 1746), p. 75.

23. Ibid., p. 105.

24. Ibid., II, p. 109.

25. Ibid., p. 114.

26. Ibid., p. 220.

27. J. B. Dubos, *Réflexions Critiques sur la poésie, la peinture et la musique* (Paris, 1719), p. 120.

28. Montesquieu, "Essai sur le goût," in *Essai sur le goût*, ed. Alexandre Gérard (Paris, 1766), p. 286.

29. Jean Joseph Taillasson, *Observations sur quelques grands peintres* (Paris, 1807), p. 63.

30. le Père Yves, *Essai sur le beau* (Paris, 1741), p. 52.

31. Publicola P. J. B. Chaussard, *Essai Philosophique sur la dignité des arts* (Paris, 1798), pp. 24, 25.

Bibliography

PRIMARY SOURCES

Where no place of publication is indicated,
Paris is to be assumed.

André, le Père Yves. *Essai sur le beau, ou l'on examine en quoi consiste précisément le beau dans le physique, dans le moral.* . . . 1741.

Arnaud, l'Abbé F., and Suard, J. B. A. *Variétés Littéraires.* 1768.

Batteux, Charles. *Les Beaux-Arts réduits à un même principe.* 1746.

Bel, J. J. "Dissertation où l'on examine le système de M. l'Abbé Dubos." In *Continuation des mémoires de littérature,* edited by Sallengre, tome III, pt. 1, pp. 3–42. 1827.

Bonnet, Charles. *Essai Analytique des facultée de l'âme.* 1717.

———. *Histoire de la misque et de ses effets.* 1715.

———. *Histoire Generale de la danse sacrée.* 1723.

Bouhours, Dominique. *La Manière de bien penser sur les ouvrages de l'esprit.* 1687.

Boye. *L'Expression Musicale.* 1778.

Briseux, C. E. *Traité du beau essentiel dans les arts.* 1752.

Cailhava de l'Estendoux, J. F. *L'Art de la comédie.* 1772.

Cartaud de la Vilate, F. *Essai Historique et Philosophique sur le goût.* Amsterdam, 1770.

Chaussard, Publicola P. J. B. "Essai Philosophique sur la dignité des arts." 1798.

Cochin, Nicolas Charles. *Les Misotechnites aux enfers.* Amsterdam, 1763.

Condillac, E. B. de. *Essai sur l'origine des connaissances humaines.* Amsterdam, 1746.

Coypel, Antoine. "Discours prononcés dans les Conférence de l'Académie Royale." 1721.

Coypel, Charles. *Discours sur la peinture.* 1749.

Crousaz, J. P. de. *Traité du beau.* Amsterdam, 1715.

Dacier, Anne Lefèbvre. *Des causes de la corruption du goût.* 1714.

Bibliography

d'Alembert, Jean. "Discours Préliminaire de l'*Encyclopédie*." 1750.

――――. "Réflexions sur l'usage et sur l'abus de la philosophie dans les matières de goût." In *Essai sur le goût*, edited by Alexandre Gérard. 1766.

d'Argens, Jean Baptiste. *La Philosophie du bon sens.* London, 1737.

――――. *Reflexions Historiques et Critiques sur le goût.* 1743.

――――. *Reflexions sur les différentes écoles de peinture.* 1751.

d'Aubignac, F. H. *La Pratique du théâtre.* 1657.

de Boissy, Charles Desprez. "Histoire des ouvrages pour et contre le théâtre." 1771.

――――. "Lettres sur les spectacles." 1759.

de Chabanon, M. P. G. *Observations sur la musique.* 1774.

――――. *Sur le sort de la poésie.* 1764.

de Chastellux, F. J. *Essai sur l'union de la poésie et de la musique.* Hague, 1765.

de Lacépède, B. G. *Poetique de la musique.* 1785.

de Marcenay de Ghuy, A. *Essai sur la beauté*, 1770.

Dezallier, Dargenville. *Abrégé de la vie des plus fameux peintres.* 1745-1752.

Diderot, Denis. *Oeuvres Esthetiques*, edited by Paul Vernière. Paris: Garnier Frères, 1959.

――――. *Oeuvres Philosophiques*, edited by Paul Vernière. Paris: Garnier Frères, 1961.

Dubos, J. B. *Réflexions Critiques sur la poésie, la peinture et la musique.* 1719.

Emeric, David. "Musée Olympique." 1796.

Estève, Pierre. *L'Esprit des beaux-arts.* 1753.

Falconet, E. M. *Oeuvres Completes.* Lausanne, 1761-1808.

Felibien, J. F. "L'Idée du peintre parfait." London, 1707.

Fontenelle, J. G. *Oeuvres Completes.* 1790.

Gérard, Alexandre de. *Essai sur le goût.* 1766.

Lacombe, Jacques. *Le Spectacle des beaux-arts.* 1758.

La Motte, A. Houdard de. *Oeuvres.* 1754 edition.

La Tour, Seran de. *L'Arts de sentir et de juger en matière de goût.* 1762.

Le Blanc, J. B. "Lettre sur l'exposition des ouvrages." 1747.

Marivaux, P. C. de. *Oeuvres Completes.* 1781.

Marmontel, Jean François. "Apologie du Théâtre." *Mercure* (November 1758).

――――. "Chefs d'oeuvres dramatiques." 1773.

――――. *Essai sur le goût.* 1786.

――――. *La Poetique française.* 1763.

Marsay, l'Abbé de. *La Peinture.* 1735.

Bibliography

Mercier, Louis Sebastien. *Du Théâtre*. Amsterdam, 1773.

Montesquieu, C. L. de S. *Esprit des lois*. Firmin-Didot Frères, 1884.

———. "Essai sur le goût." In *Essai sur le goût*, edited by Alexandre Gérard. 1766.

Piles, Roger de. *Conversation sur la connaissance de la peinture*. 1708.

———. *Cours de peinture*. 1708.

———. *Diverses Conversations sur la peinture*. 1777.

Poinsinet de Sivry, L. "Traité des causes physiques et morales du rire." Amsterdam, 1768.

Ponce, Nicolas. "De l'influence de la nature." 1797.

Quincy, A. de. *Considerations sur les arts du dessin en France*. 1791.

———. *Dictionnaire d'architecture*. 1789.

———. *Letter au Général Miranda*. 1796.

Racine, Louis. *Réflexions sur la poésie*. 1752.

Rémond de Saint-Mard, T. *Lettres sur la décadence du goût en France*. 1733.

———. *Réflexions sur l'opéra*. 1743.

Reymond, George Marie. *De la peinture*. 1799.

Rollin, Charles. *De la manière d'enseigner et d'étudier les belles-lettres*. 1726–1728.

Rousseau, Jean Jacques. *Oeuvres*, edited by Didier. 1834.

Saint-Evremond, C. de. *Oeuvres*, edited by Desmaizeaux. 1705.

Saint-Yonne, La Font de. *Réflexions sur quelques causes de L'État présent de la peinture en France*. Hague, 1747.

———. *Sentiments sur quelques ouvrages de peinture*. 1752.

Stael-Holstein, A. L. G. *Essai sur les fictions*. Lausanne, 1795.

Taillasson, Jean Joseph. "Le Danger des règles dans les arts. . . ." 1785.

———. *Observations sur quelques grands peintres. . . .* 1807.

Trublet, l'Abbé N. C. J. *Essais sur divers sujets de littérature et de morale*. Amsterdam, 1755.

Villoteau, G. A. *Recherchés sur l'analogie de la musique. . . .* 1785.

Voltaire, F. M. A. de. *Oeuvres Completes (Siècle* edition). 1867–1873.

Watelet, C. H. *Dictionnaire des beaux-arts*. 1788.

SELECTED SECONDARY SOURCES

Bayer, Raymond. *Histoire de l'esthetique*. Paris: Armand Colin, 1961.

Belaval, Yvon. *L'Esthetique sans paradoxe de Diderot*. Paris: Gallimard, 1950.

Boas, George. "The Arts in the *Encyclopédie*." *The Journal of Aesthetics and Art Criticism*, 23, no. 1 (Fall 1964), pp. 97–107.

Bibliography

Bosanquet, B. *A History of Aesthetics.* London: Sonnenscheim, 1892.
Cassirer, Ernst. *The Philosophy of the Enlightenment.* Princeton, N. J.: Princeton University Press, 1951.
Crocker, L. G. *The Age of Crisis: Man and World in Eighteenth-Century French Thought.* Baltimore, Md.: Johns Hopkins University Press, 1959.
————. *Nature and Culture: Ethical Thought in the Enlightenment.* Baltimore, Md.: Johns Hopkins University Press, 1963.
————. *Two Diderot Studies: Ethics and Aesthetics.* Baltimore, Md.: Johns Hopkins University Press, 1952.
Dieckmann, Herbert. *Cinq Leçons sur Diderot.* Geneva: Droz, 1959.
————. *Diderot und Goldoni.* Krefeld, Germany: Scherpe Verlag, 1961.
Fellowes, Otis E., and Torrey, Norman L., eds. *Diderot Studies.* Vols. I-II. Syracuse, N. Y.: Syracuse University Press, 1949-1952.
Fellowes, Otis E., and May, Gita eds. *Diderot Studies.* Vol. III. Geneva: Droz, 1961.
Fellowes, Otis E., ed. *Diderot Studies.* Vol. IV. Geneva: Droz, 1963.
Folkierski, Wladyslaw. *Entre le classicisme et le romantisme.* Paris: Librairie Ancienne Honoré Champio, 1925.
Fontaine, André. *Les Doctrines d'art en France, de Poussin à Diderot.* Paris: Champion, 1909.
Gaxotte, Pierre. *Paris au XVIIIᵉ siècle.* Paris: Arthaud, 1968.
Gilbert, Katherine, and Kuhn, Helmut. *A History of Aesthetics.* New York: Macmillan, 1939.
Gillot, Hubert. *Denis Diderot.* Paris: G. Courville, 1937.
Glotz, Marguerite, and Maire, Madeleine. *Les Salons du XVIIIᵉ siècle.* Paris: Nouville Editions Latines, 1949.
May, Georges. *Diderot et Baudelaire critiques d'art.* Geneva: Droz, 1957.
————. *Quatre Visages de Denis Diderot.* Paris: Boivin, 1950.
Mustoxidi, T. M. *Histoire de l'esthetique française, 1700-1900.* Paris: Edouard Champion, 1920.
Pomeau, René. *Diderot.* Paris: Presses Universitaires de France, 1967.
Reau, Louis. *Le Rayonnement de Paris au XVIIIᵉ siècle.* 6th ed. Dijon, France: Robert Lafont, 1946.
Saintsbury, George. *History of Criticism and Literary Taste in Europe.* London: Routledge and Kegan Paul, 1902.
Saisselin, R. G. *Taste in Eighteenth-Century France.* Syracuse, N. Y.: Syracuse University Press, 1965.
Schneider, R. *L'Art Français: XVIIIᵉ siècle.* Paris: Laurens, 1926.
Van Tieghem, Phillippe. *Petite Histoire des grandes doctrines littéraires en France.* Paris: Presses Universitaires de France, 1954.

Index

Aesthetic happiness: in Diderot, 132-36

Aesthetic rules: characteristics of, 51-54; general attitudes toward, 54-60, 68, 143. *See also* subdivision *on aesthetic rules* under specific names of philosophers

Aesthetic theory: distinguished from critical theory, xiv-xv, 33. *See also* subdivision *aesthetics of* under specific names of philosophers

Aesthetic value: in Batteux, 63; in Diderot, 132-33; in Dubos, 31-32; in Marcenay de Ghuy, 85

Alembert, J. d': mentioned, 33; on taste, 36-38

André, Yves: aesthetics of, 28-31; mentioned, xiii, 47; on aesthetic rules, 83-84; on value of art, 146

Argens, J. B. d': on aesthetic rules, 73; on taste, 31

Art: moral function of, 145-48; origin of, 137-41; rules of, 141-43; value in experience of, 132-36, 144-45

Art vs. nature: 94-105

Batteux, C.: aesthetics of, 23-27; mentioned, xiii, xvii, xviii, 47, 82; on aesthetic rules, 60-67; on art as imitation of nature, 94-97, 98, 105; on value of art, 144-45

Baumgarten, A. G.: mentioned, xviii

Beauty: André on, 28-29; Batteux on, 23-24, 27; Briseux on, 50-51; Crousaz on, 6-14, 29, 105; Descartes on, 6; Diderot on, 41-46, 87; Dubos on, 15-17, 29-30; Estève on, 21; Marcenay de Ghuy on, 50, 84-85; Piles on, 101; Trublet on, 18-19

Bonnet, C.: aesthetics of, 21-22

Bouhours, D.: mentioned, 49

Briseux, C. E.: definition of beauty of, 50-51; on aesthetic rules, 68-69

Bullough, E.: mentioned, 107

Chaussard, P.: on the value of art, 146-47

Condillac, E. B. de: mentioned, xvii, 33; on origin of art, 138-40; on origin of language, 137-38

Creativity. *See* Originality

Critical theory: distinguished from aesthetic theory, xiv-xv

Crocker, L. G.: cited, xiv

Crousaz, J. P. de: aesthetics of, 6-14, 29; mentioned, xiii, xvii, xviii, 31, 49; on aesthetic rules, 50, 82-83;

Index

Taillasson, J. J.: on aesthetic rules, 72-73; on function of art, 145; on imitation of nature, 99-101

Taste: definitions of, 21, 23-24, 26, 31-35, 39-40, 64, 85, 106-07; effects of, 29, 87; theories of, 9, 14, 16, 18-20, 36-38, 63

Tragedy: Pleasure in, 106-09

Trublet, N. C. J.: aesthetics of, xix, 17-19; on aesthetic rules, xvii, 81-82; on art as imitation of nature, 93-94

Ugly in art: 101-02, 105-09

Voltaire, F. M. A. de: aesthetics of, 34-36; mentioned, xvi, 33, 100

Winckelmann, J. J.: mentioned, 48

Wolff, C.: mentioned, xviii